D1070842

A's
ESSENTIAL

Everything You Need to Know to Be a Real Fan!

Steven Travers

TRIUMPH
BOOKS

Library of Congress Cataloging-in-Publication Data

Travers, Steven.
    A's essential : everything you need to know to be a real fan! / Steven Travers.
        p. cm.
    Includes bibliographical references.
    ISBN-13: 978-1-57243-926-9
    ISBN-10: 1-57243-926-2
    1. Oakland Athletics (Baseball team)—History. 2. Baseball—California—Oakland—History. I. Title.

GV875.O24T73 2007
796.357'640979466—dc22

                                        2006028184

This book is available in quantity at special discounts for your group or organization. For further information, contact:

Triumph Books
542 South Dearborn Street
Suite 750
Chicago, Illinois 60605
(312) 939-3330
Fax (312) 663-3557

Printed in U.S.A.
ISBN: 978-1-57243-926-9
Design by Patricia Frey
All photos courtesy of Ron Riesterer except where otherwise indicated

To my dad
because you were never tired when I wanted to practice,
because of all those A's games you took me to,
and because we shared baseball
memories more precious than gold.
Thank you.

Contents

Foreword

The American League started in 1901, and in the century since that time, the Athletics franchise has gone through ups and downs, which include stays in Philadelphia, Kansas City, and now Oakland. Throughout all those ups and downs, the A's have been one of the great dynasties in the American sports pantheon.

Nine times the A's have brought home the coveted world championship. And all those years Hall of Famers have dotted the A's roster: Lefty Grove, Jimmie Foxx, Jimmy Dykes, and Mickey Cochrane are all-time legends. Manager Connie Mack liked college players such as Eddie Collins, Chief Bender, and Eddie Plank, and I have found college players to be a reliable part of our scouting process, too.

In Oakland, the A's helped to develop the East Bay's winning identity, turning the Coliseum into the "Home of Champions." As great as Mack's A's were, it could be argued that in Oakland this franchise has seen its most profound glory. Reggie, Cap'n Sal, Vida. Oh, what memories.

Steve Travers has captured it all in *A's Essential*, an anecdotal, fun read that tells you all you need to know about the franchise's best teams, most exciting players, record-breaking superstars, and colorful characters. You'll read about Rube Waddell, who soaked his arm in ice *before* the game to "take the speed off"; Ken "Hawk" Harrelson, who became baseball's first free agent after playing in Kansas City; and the legendary Charlie O. Finley, who had an uncanny knack for spotting talented players in out-of-the-way places, not to mention giving them nicknames like "Catfish," "Blue Moon," and "Jumbo Jim."

I am very proud to be associated with a team with such a winning tradition, a team so important to the game of baseball and to the fans of the Bay Area. It is said that baseball is the best game to write about, so delightful are its stories. It is also a statistics-oriented game in which comparisons of players and teams over the course of seasons and careers somehow work in ways they do not in other sports. And it makes for great reading, too. For some reason, over the years the languid, everyday pace of baseball has made our national pastime the source of our best sportswriting. The color, the humor, the ambience—each team has its own identity. Some teams are corporate in nature. Others are considered straightlaced or All-American. Others are teams of pathos or disappointment. The A's are unique in their sense of true color, of unique character. These traits have followed the team from the days of Rube Waddell to Reggie Jackson to Barry Zito.

It is all here in *A's Essential:* the trivia, the numbers, the stories, the pure flavor of A's baseball, in all its varied and wonderful brands over the years. As you read this book, let's hope the best is still to come.

—Billy Beane
A's general manager

Acknowledgments

Thanks to Tom Bast, Jess Paumier, Amy Reagan, Kelley White, Linc Wonham, and all the great folks at Triumph Books and Random House Publishing for having faith in me. Thanks also to my agent, Craig Wiley. I want to thank the Oakland A's, a class organization all the way, and Ron Riesterer of *The Oakland Tribune* for all his great photos. Thanks also to Pat Kelly and John Horne of the Baseball Hall of Fame and to Bruce Seltzer, amateur photographer and great Trojan!

I would further like to thank Karen Peterson for her technical help. Also, thank you to Debbie Gallas, Mike Selleck, and Michael Young of the A's. I also want to extend my gratitude to Billy Beane, general manager of the A's, for all his help. Thank you to Marty Lurie and Shooty Babitt, too. Thank you to Barry Zito, Tim Hudson, Mark Mulder, Jason Giambi, Johnny Damon, Mark McGwire, Jose Canseco, Ken Korach, Ray Fosse, Tony La Russa, Art Howe, and Ken Macha. Thanks to the late Bill King and the late Bill Rigney. Thank you to Bruce Macgowan.

Of course, my thanks as always go out to my daughter, Elizabeth Travers; my parents, Don and Inge Travers; and to my Lord and savior, Jesus Christ, who has shed his grace on thee, and to whom all glory is due!

Introduction:
A Father and a Son;
a Game and a Team

The team had funny green and gold uniforms. They wore white shoes. A mule presided over the pregame sidelines. They had a bunch of young guys with new names: Rudi, Bando, Fingers, Jackson, Campaneris, Lindblad, Hunter, Odom, Pagliaroni, and Nash. Their announcer talked funny, using words like *phantasmagoric*.

I loved 'em. My father and I went to about 35 games a year. No memories are more precious than night games in the summer, followed by a late meal at Marin Joe's. We went to all the playoff and World Series games. Over the years, I went to hundreds of games with my dad, sometimes with my mom, right on up to the 2000s. Eventually I was able to share the experience with my daughter, Elizabeth.

My dad was always there for me. I never, ever, *not one single time,* asked my dad to practice baseball with me and heard him say, "Oh, not today," or "I'm too tired," or "I'm busy." Never once, and it was not like I wanted to practice once a week or so. I was *into it.*

I went to Redwood High School in Marin, California. One of my teammates was Buddy Biancalana, who later became the starting shortstop for the 1985 world champion Kansas City Royals. In 1977 the Redwood Giants were undefeated and ranked number one in California when we ventured to Ted Williams Field in San Diego. Ted Williams had indeed starred at Hoover High School. We led 5–3 entering the bottom of the seventh in a seven-inning game, but Hoover loaded the bases. We brought in Buddy to pitch. He normally did not take the mound, but we had used up most of our staff and he threw hard.

Mike Davis hit a triple off Buddy to give the Hoover Cardinals a 6–5 victory, ending our unbeaten streak. That was the same Mike

Davis who later played for the A's and, as a member of the Dodgers, drew a walk from Dennis Eckersley, setting up Kirk Gibson's "miracle" home run to win Game 1 of the 1988 World Series! We also had a lively rivalry going with the Berkeley Yellowjackets, whose star shortstop was future Oakland A Shooty Babitt.

That Redwood team won the national championship. Perhaps the second best team in America that year was El Camino Real High School of south San Francisco. Their ace pitcher was a 6'7" right-hander who later starred at Fresno State and pitched for the A's: Rich Bordi. All season *The* (San Francisco) *Examiner* detailed our exploits as El Camino Real won the CIF-Central Coast Section title and we won the North Coast Section championship. A prospective "national championship game" between us, to be played at Candlestick Park or the Oakland Coliseum, was nixed for insurance reasons.

I pitched in the St. Louis Cardinals organization, where I was a teammate of future A's outfielder Stanley Javier at Johnson City, Tennessee, of the Appalachian League. In 1981 I beat the Kingsport (Tennessee) Mets, 8–4, striking out a league-record 14 batters. Three of those strikeouts came against Kevin Mitchell, later the 1989 National League Most Valuable Player and a member of the A's in 1998.

In 1982 my dreams were further realized when I was signed by the Oakland A's. That spring the A's featured a veteran minor league catcher named Darryl Cias. He was the Crash Davis character from *Bull Durham,* and hardcore A's fans will remember that in 1983 Cias got called up to Oakland and played 19 games.

I actually pitched in a major league exhibition game, on a Saturday afternoon before a nice crowd, and both the A's and Giants broadcast it back to the Bay Area—to my hometown! The A's manager was Billy Martin. The pitching coach was Art Fowler. Martin said nothing to me. I pitched the fourth, fifth, and sixth innings. Rickey Henderson was in left field. Shooty Babitt played shortstop. Mickey Tettleton was the catcher. Nine up, nine down. Five or six strikeouts. I was unhittable.

Later I heard from friends who listened to Bill King and Lon Simmons describe my three innings on the A's broadcast. I am told

King even did some research, mentioning that I was "a Marin County product"—King lived there, too—"who starred at Redwood High in their glory days."

Glory days they were, but they were short-lived. I made a very brief stop at Modesto of the Class A California League, where current A's coach Brad Fischer was at the time. I was there long enough to throw batting practice.

Then they sent me to Idaho Falls, where the manager was current A's director of minor league development Keith Lieppman, and his coach was former A's executive Grady Fuson.

Some of my teammates made names for themselves. Dave Wilder later was traded to the Cubs for Dennis Eckersley and is now a top executive with Milwaukee. Jose Canseco was a young farmhand at Idaho Falls that year, too.

In 1991 I coached on Bob Milano's baseball staff at the University of California. We played an exhibition game against the A's at the Oakland Coliseum prior to their season opener. My USC classmate Mark McGwire saw me in a Cal uniform and exclaimed, "What in the world are you doing wearing that?" A's manager Tony La Russa was exceptionally generous with his time, speaking to the Cal coaches during batting practice. Jose Canseco, wearing a muscle shirt, put on a machismo batting practice display while engaging in running commentary/bravado with Dave Henderson. The A's looked much more like a football team than a baseball team. Dave Stewart started and introduced his new forkball. The Cal hitters—and this might have been the best offensive team in college baseball that year— were utterly befuddled. The difference between college and major league pitching was incredible!

As a Los Angeles columnist, I covered Barry Zito at USC. I also wrote a screenplay about the late Angels playboy Bo Belinsky. Bo's manager, Bill Rigney, who also passed away, was a longtime A's executive. He was very helpful to me.

To quote a character from *Saturday Night Live,* "Beisbol been very, very good to me," and no team has given my dad and me greater joy than the A's.

Mr. Mack

The Athletics franchise has been in Oakland since 1968, but long before they played on the West Coast, and before they were the Kansas City A's in the 1950s and '60s, the A's played in Philadelphia. The face of the team was Connie Mack.

They do not make 'em like Connie Mack anymore—not in baseball, and seemingly not anywhere in society. Mack was a gentleman, a grandfatherly type, referred to not as Skip or Connie or Cap, but as Mr. Mack, by players, umpires, opponents, fans.

He did not wear a uniform. Instead he wore a full suit, starched collar, tie, dress shoes, the whole nine yards. Day games in Philly, New York, Washington, D.C., in the summer time, when the heat and humidity are unbearable. Only every once in a great while, when the temperatures hovered around 100 degrees and the sweat made shirts stick to bodies like glue, would Mr. Mack take off his coat, possibly loosen his tie. Toward the end, he would nod off in the corner of the dugout.

Mack is a monumental figure in baseball history. One of the nicest fellows ever, the anti–Ty Cobb. He was born Cornelius McGillicuddy in East Brookfield, Massachusetts, in 1862, right in the middle of the Civil War. His parents were Irish immigrants. Cornelius's Christianity was a major part of his upbringing and demeanor throughout his life. He was loved by everyone who ever knew him.

"A truly religious man," Rube Bressler, who pitched for him before World War I, told Lawrence S. Ritter in the remarkable 1966 classic *The Glory of Their Times.* "I mean *really* religious. Not a hypocrite...

That in 1930 Connie Mack was the recipient of the Bok Award, a tribute that carried with it an embossed scroll, a medal, and $10,000 for having rendered greatest service to the city of Philadelphia in the preceding year?

"In my opinion, Connie Mack did more for baseball than any other living human being—by the example he set, his attitude, the way he handled himself and his players."

McGillicuddy resembled an Anglican pastor from England. In an age in which ballplayers were alcoholics, gamblers, whoremongers, and reprobates, McGillicuddy was straight up and down, engendering respect from his players and opponents alike.

His name was so long that one and all knew him as Connie Mack. He was an excellent catcher in his own right and then in 1901 became the founding owner and manager of the brand-new Philadelphia franchise in the fledgling American League.

Despite Mack's visage and the fact that he symbolizes the old-time values of baseball, he in fact was one of the first owners to break up his team for financial reasons—which he did not once but twice.

After winning the American League pennant four out of five years between 1910 and 1914, Mack sold all his stars to pay the bills. World War I had broken out in Europe, and the Federal League raided his and other teams of top talent.

Mack again built a dynasty from 1929 to 1931, winning two World Series and three straight American League championships, but the Great Depression dragged attendance down, causing him to sell all his stars again, many of whom were Hall of Famers.

Billy Beane would have loved Mack's style.

"Mr. Mack began replacing age with youth from what is called the 'free-agency' field," wrote his friend and fellow legend, Branch Rickey, in his marvelous 1965 book of baseball nuggets, *The American Diamond*. "In that day good colleges offered the most prospects, and Mr. Mack signed a number of players directly from college. Among these were Eddie Plank from Gettysburg College; Chief Bender, Carlisle Indian School; Eddie Collins, Columbia University; Jack Barry, Holy Cross; and Jack Coombs, Colby College."

Connie Mack's A's gave respectability to the American League at a time when it needed to establish itself. The National League had operated since 1876. The AL—known forevermore as the "junior circuit"—was formed out of the American Association and expansion franchises in 1901.

In 1904 the second World Series between the Boston Pilgrims (later Red Sox)—the surprise winners of the first Series in 1903—and John McGraw's New York Giants was canceled. McGraw refused to play "bushers." In 1905 McGraw was persuaded to play Mack's championship A's. Christy Mathewson proved McGraw right by twirling three shutouts as the Giants dominated Philadelphia.

In the 1900s the National League was stronger, but Mack's A's won the 1910, 1911, and 1913 World Series. In 1914 they were favored but lost to the Miracle Braves, who went from last place on July 4 to the world championship.

Mack's ace pitchers were Rube Waddell and Charles "Chief" Bender. Bender

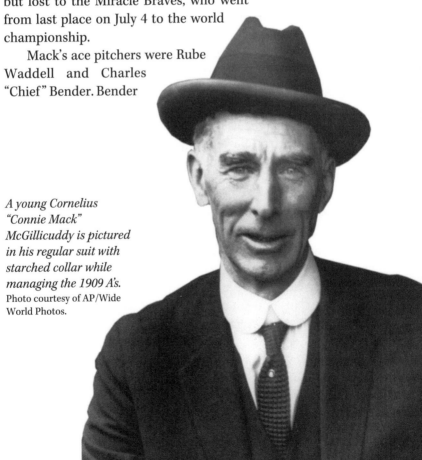

A young Cornelius "Connie Mack" McGillicuddy is pictured in his regular suit with starched collar while managing the 1909 A's. Photo courtesy of AP/Wide World Photos.

By the
NUMBERS
3,731–3,948 (.486)—Connie Mack's lifetime managerial record with the Pittsburgh National League club from 1894 to 1896, then the Philadelphia A's (he was part owner, too) from 1901 to 1950. He managed in eight World Series, winning five, with an overall Series record of 24–19.

was an American Indian who, like the great Jim Thorpe, had attended Carlisle.

"One of the finest and kindest men who ever lived," said Bressler of Bender, who roomed with him.

The A's featured the famed "$100,000 infield" of first baseman Stuffy McInnis, second baseman Eddie Collins, third baseman Frank "Home Run" Baker, and shortstop Jack Barry. After losing to the Braves, Collins was traded to Chicago for $50,000. Barry and pitching sensation Herb Pennock were traded to Boston, forming the next dynasty that would team up with Babe Ruth. Baker and Bob Shawkey were traded to the Yankees and Jack Coombs went to Brooklyn, while Bender and another pitching great, Eddie Plank, jumped to the Federal League.

Mack's A's were mediocre for almost 15 years, but in the late 1920s they again emerged as a contender with a new class of young stars. By that point the New York Yankees of Babe Ruth and Lou Gehrig had dominated baseball for a decade, but in 1928 pitcher Lefty Grove was the best in the game; he was the only hurler who could stop Murderer's Row.

The 1929 A's are regarded as one of the best teams in baseball history. They had to be in order to wrest the title from the Yankees. Grove and George Earnshaw were 20-game winners. First baseman Jimmie Foxx slammed 33 home runs. Left fielder Al Simmons hit 34 homers and drove in 157 runs. Catcher Mickey Cochrane batted .331. The team won an incredible 104 games against 46 defeats, then squared off against the Chicago Cubs in the World Series.

In the opener at Wrigley Field, Mack surprised everyone by holding back Grove and Earnshaw in favor of 35-year-old journeyman pitcher Howard Ehmke. Ehmke came through, stopping Chicago 3–1 and setting a Series record by striking out 13 Cubs.

In the fourth game, at Shibe Park in Philadelphia, Chicago led 8–0 through six and a half innings, but the A's rallied. When the Cubs' erstwhile center fielder Hack Wilson lost a fly ball in the sun, it resulted in an inside-the-park three-run homer. Eventually Philadelphia prevailed, 10–8, en route to a 4–1 Series win.

Later that month Black Monday hit. The stock market tumbled, and the Great Depression was on. The A's dominated American League play in 1930 and 1931. They defeated St. Louis in the 1930 World Series but were upset by the famed Gashouse Gang in 1931. In that 1931 campaign, Grove recorded one of the best

TRIVIA

When Connie Mack entered the Hall of Fame in 1937, did he do so as a player or a manager?

Answers to the trivia questions are on pages 196–198.

seasons in history, winning 31 games against four losses with a 2.06 earned-run average. Al Simmons hit .390 in 1931.

But the economy was so bad that Mack was forced to sell off most of his team, bit by bit, over the next couple of seasons. The Yankees ownership was able to withstand the times, retaining their stars and continuing to win throughout the decade. But Mack sold or traded no less than five future Hall of Famers: Grove, Foxx, Cochrane, Simmons, and Jimmy Dykes.

Grove and Foxx starred for Boston. Cochrane led Detroit to glory. Dykes became the manager of the Chicago White Sox. Foxx became a bad alcoholic. (The Tom Hanks character from *A League of Their Own* is loosely based on Foxx.) Cochrane lost his son in World War II and reportedly never recovered.

Mack's A's did not return to greatness, even though he managed the team until 1950.

Rube and Mack's First Champions

The anchor of Connie Mack's first great champions was George Edward "Rube" Waddell, and what a rube he was!

Born on October 13, 1876, in Bradford, Pennsylvania, Waddell broke into professional baseball with Louisville of the National League in 1897. The Louisville club of the late 1890s became the Pittsburgh Pirates. The great superstar Honus Wagner anchored the team.

After starting the 1902 season with a strong showing, pitching for the Los Angeles club of the Pacific Coast League, Waddell was purchased by Mack. The fledgling A's and the new American League were still establishing themselves amid competition with the National League, a situation not unlike the AFL's struggle for equality with pro football's NFL in the 1960s.

The 6'1", 196-pound left-hander was just what the doctor ordered, as he immediately won 24 games in the remainder of the 1902 season. Waddell followed that with 21 wins in 1903, then 25 (1904) and 27 (1905). In 1904 Rube struck out between 343 and 349 batters. The figures are disputed, as records were not as well kept then, but nevertheless he held the all-time single-season strikeout mark until Sandy Koufax broke it in 1965 (Bob Feller of Cleveland struck out 348 in 1946).

Rube must be considered one of the hardest-throwing pitchers of all time. Prior to Rube, Denton "Cy" Young was considered the fastest of pitchers. A short list of all-time heaterballers includes Young, Waddell, Walter "Big Train" Johnson, Lefty Grove, Bob Feller, Steve Dalkowski (who never pitched in the majors), Sandy Koufax, Tom Seaver, Nolan Ryan, Roger Clemens, and Randy Johnson. This is a *very* exclusive list.

Rube Waddell, a wild and colorful character, held the single-season strikeout record of 349 until Sandy Koufax broke the mark with 382 in 1965. Photo courtesy of Getty Images.

6—The number of consecutive years Rube Waddell led the American League in strikeouts. In an era in which players bunted, choked up, and hit for contact, he K'd 210 (1902), 302 (1903), 349 (1904), 287 (1905), 196 (1906), and 226 (1907) hitters.

Mack's 1905 A's were the first of his championship teams. Rube was not able to maintain a long, great career, however. His 193 wins fall far short of his potential.

Even though Mr. Mack was not a college man himself, his professorial demeanor made college players attractive to him and vice versa. But Mack's players were not all Ivy League preppies. He had his share of characters. None more full of character than the otherwise-sensational Waddell, who, although never medically diagnosed, was believed to be mentally unbalanced. Left-handed baseball pitchers have always been thought to be flaky. Lefty "el Goofy" Gomez and Bill "Spaceman" Lee fostered the image, but Waddell was the first one—the original flaky southpaw.

Waddell claimed on some days to "have so much speed today I'll burn up the catcher's mitt if I don't let up a bit," so he would ice his arm *before* the game.

"Wahoo Sam" Crawford and Hall of Famer Ty Cobb were teammates in Detroit. Waddell had monumental battles facing the three-time American League champion (1907–09) Tigers of Crawford and Cobb. Crawford was a minor league teammate of Waddell's before becoming an opponent.

"Rube would just disappear," Crawford recalled.

The pitcher would not show up for his scheduled start until game time. He would be "off playing ball with a bunch of 12-year-olds in an empty lot somewhere," continued Crawford. "The manager would be having a fit.... And then just a few minutes before game time there'd be a commotion in the grandstand and you'd hear people laughing and yelling: 'Here comes Rube, here comes Rube.'"

Waddell would change into his uniform while crossing the field—"He never wore underwear," said Crawford—and in three minutes he would be ready. Waddell drove Mr. Mack to distraction.

At the slightest provocation he would literally wander off the field. If a fire engine roared by, he would leave the game to check it out. It was Mack who thought his Christian charity and pious influence would straighten out the giant Rube. In fact, that is precisely what allowed Rube the chance to achieve the fleeting greatness he did have, after years in the minors. Other managers were not willing to take a chance with him until Mack finally did.

Even when Mack decided to sign Rube, he had to send two weeks' worth of telegrams before Rube replied, "Come and get me." Mack paid off Rube's debts and rescued his belongings from a hockshop.

In 1904 Waddell and Young hooked up in one of baseball's best-ever pitcher's duels. It took a perfect game by Young to beat Rube, but the next year Waddell defeated Young, 3–2, in a 12-inning barn burner.

Waddell also had a huge curve, known as a bender. Mack said he possessed "more throwing ability than anybody I've ever seen."

Mack also had Eddie Plank and young Chief Bender on that 1905 club.

Rube was a raging alcoholic who experienced many a "lost weekend." It all caught up to him, of course. His career was cut short, and Rube died an early death.

Tragic death via alcohol was not particularly unusual for some of baseball's early ballplayers. Another Philadelphia star was Ed Delahanty of the Phillies. He came from a big Irish family. Most of his brothers made it to the major leagues, but Ed was the star, a Hall of Famer who batted .346 for his lifetime.

Delahanty went from Philadelphia to Washington, and in July of 1903 the team was traveling through upstate New York by train. According to lore, Delahanty was intoxicated when the train

IF ONLY . . . Rube Waddell had not been injured and forced to sit out the 1905 World Series, the A's might have fared better than losing in five games to the Giants. All five games were shutouts: three by New York's Christy Mathewson, one by the Giants' Joe McGinnity, and the lone Philadelphia win coming on Chief Bender's whitewashing of the Giants in Game 2.

stopped at the famous Niagara Falls. Nobody knows for sure what happened, but witnesses said Delahanty was seen stumbling around near the guardrail. Then, just like that, he was gone. Nobody actually saw him go over the side, but it was determined that in a state of drunkenness he somehow fell—or even climbed—over the guardrails, slipped, and fell to a spectacular death in the mists below.

Delahanty and Waddell represent tragic tales of baseball's early days, days in which players came from small towns far and wide, were exposed to big city enticements, and fell prey to them.

The baseball experience could be compared to little else, and in the early 20th century there was no template for how to handle fame and money. Perhaps the experiences of rural Americans going off to fight in the Civil War and later World War I could be comparable. Few players had traveled much beyond their hometowns. Certainly there were not many with college backgrounds (with some notable exceptions). It was even hit or miss that they would have played high school baseball. Some players, if they were from cities like San Francisco, Los Angeles, New York, or Boston, probably played in high school, but others were educated in one-room schoolhouses on the prairie, where an outhouse was luxurious and a baseball diamond almost unheard of.

They came up in a rough 'n' tumble manner, through semipro, town ball, and a minor league "system" that was one part "gun fight at the OK corral" and one part *Huck Finn*. It was all adventure, the growth of America, and these characters were uniquely part of the fabric of a young nation.

Baseball's First Dynasty

In the first decade of the 20th century, many great teams emerged. John McGraw's New York Giants were led by the pitching combination of Christy Mathewson and "Iron Joe" McGinnity. The Pittsburgh Pirates were led by the great shortstop Honus Wagner. The famed double-play combination of Tinker-to-Evers-to-Chance formed the nucleus of the Cubs' *last* world championship (1908).

In the American League, a battle for supremacy developed among Ty Cobb's Detroit Tigers, who won three straight American League pennants (1907 through 1909); the Boston Red Sox, winners of the first-ever World Series in 1903; the Chicago White Sox, known as the "Hitless Wonders" of 1906; and Connie Mack's A's.

Throughout the decade the World Series was marked by upsets more often than not. The result was that no single team emerged as a consistent champion, until Mack's A's dynasty of 1910 to 1914. Philadelphia won three World Series (1910, 1911, and 1913) but lost the fourth in another upset to the Miracle Braves.

The team's superstar was Hall of Fame second baseman Eddie Collins. A product of the Ivy League, Collins was an all-around player who could hit, run, and field with the best of them. In 1909 he hit .346.

The league's superstars in the early 1910s were Cobb and "Shoeless Joe" Jackson of the White Sox, along with many great pitchers who dominated the dead-ball era. The era was so named because the ball did not travel far and pitchers were allowed to throw spitters, shine balls, licorice balls, emory balls, and "nick" balls. But Collins was as steady as anybody. He also won more than Cobb or Jackson. In 1910 he batted .322 with 81 stolen bases. He

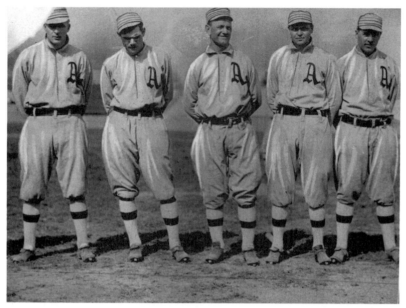

Pictured, from left, are Rube Oldring, Eddie Murphy, Danny Murphy, Amos Strunk, and Jimmy Walsh of the 1913 world champion Philadelphia A's.
Photo courtesy of AP/Wide World Photos.

finished his career with 3,315 hits and was elected to Cooperstown in 1939.

But Collins's winning ways were also due to his marvelous teammates: the "$100,000 infield" of Collins, Frank Baker, Stuffy McInnis, Jack Barry, and Harry Davis, along with pitching stalwarts Jack Coombs and Chief Bender. The 1910 A's dominated with a 102–48 mark, then dismantled the Cubs in the fall classic.

In 1911 they ran the table by 13½ games over Cobb's Tigers. John McGraw, one of the most superstitious baseball men ever, got it in his mind that his Giants needed to wear black uniforms in the Series because they had worn black when they beat the 1905 A's. The Series also featured something fairly rare for major league baseball at the time: two full-blooded Native Americans.

The A's had Bender, and the Giants had Chief Meyers as their catcher. Meyers was a Californian who had attended Dartmouth, which was founded as an Indian school and to this day awards scholarships to academically qualified Native Americans. Two years later

Meyers's teammate would be the Native American Jim Thorpe, possibly the best athlete of all time. A college football All-American at Carlisle, Thorpe won the gold medal in the pentathlon (now known as the decathlon) at the 1912 Stockholm Olympics, then played a few years for the Giants. In the 1920s he played in the fledgling National Football League.

McGraw, a gruff, coarse man, nevertheless was ahead of his time when it came to minorities. Aside from playing two Native Americans, it is little known that the first black player ever was not really Jackie Robinson. McGraw employed at least two black players in the 1900s, passing them off as Cubans or Puerto Ricans until the ruse was discovered. One of them was Jose Mendez.

The A's, of course, featured the fabulous Bender. Bender had been in Rube Waddell's shadow from 1902 to 1908, but after Waddell wore out his welcome, Chief assumed the mantel of staff ace, going 23–5 in 1910, 17–5 in 1911, 21–10 in 1913, and 17–3 in 1914. He won two games each in the 1911 and 1913 World Series. Earned-run averages were not kept until 1913, when he compiled a 2.21 ERA. His 2.75 lifetime ERA would have been lower had it included his great years from 1903 (when he broke into the majors straight out of Carlisle) to 1912. (Editor's note: Historians have gone back and reconstructed ERAs prior to 1913, giving Bender a 2.46 ERA.) He was a dominant pitcher, although his records are overshadowed by even more spectacular contemporaries, including Walter Johnson of Washington, "Smoky Joe" Wood of Boston (for one brief year, 1912), and Grover Cleveland Alexander of the Phillies, plus Waddell, Mathewson, and McGinnity.

Bender made the mistake of going to the Federal League in 1915, where for unexplained reasons he was only 4–16. He pitched in organized ball off and on, but his lifetime 212 wins could have been more had he stayed the course. In 1953 he was elected to the Hall of Fame.

In Game 2 of the 1911 Series against Rube Marquard, who had won an incredible 24 straight games for the Giants, Frank Baker's home

TRIVIA

How did Connie Mack come to be the owner of the Philadelphia A's?

Answers to the trivia questions are on pages 196–198.

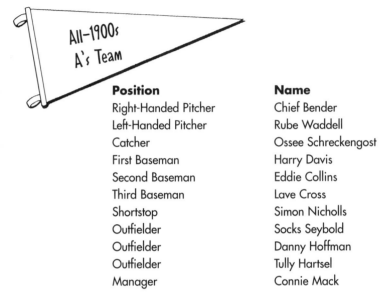

All-1900s A's Team

Position	Name
Right-Handed Pitcher	Chief Bender
Left-Handed Pitcher	Rube Waddell
Catcher	Ossee Schreckengost
First Baseman	Harry Davis
Second Baseman	Eddie Collins
Third Baseman	Lave Cross
Shortstop	Simon Nicholls
Outfielder	Socks Seybold
Outfielder	Danny Hoffman
Outfielder	Tully Hartsel
Manager	Connie Mack

run was the margin of victory. The next game pitted Mack's crew against the incredible Mathewson. Coombs dueled him to a 1–1 tie until Baker came up in the ninth. Matty appeared to have struck him out, but the umpire ruled a tip, giving him life. On the next pitch he homered. The A's won the game. Homers on successive days were so rare for the dead-ball era that Baker became forever known as "Home Run" Baker, one of the best nicknames ever achieved. It probably made the difference in his getting elected to the Hall in 1955.

The 1913 World Series was a rematch with a touch of old and new. The new were two phenoms added to Mack's roster: pitching stars "Bullet Joe" Bush and Hall of Famer Herb Pennock. The old was the same Giants team with Matty and Marquard, this time sporting a 19-game winning streak. It was not close. A's in five.

After the Boston Braves defeated Philadelphia in the 1914 World Series, however, the new Federal League and war in Europe created different sets of problems for Mack, but the overall effect was that his $100,000 infield had become financially unfeasible. The team was traded, mainly to the Red Sox, baseball's next dynasty until Ruth's Yankees.

A Rube by Any Other Name

Why is it that in the beginning of the 20th century, everybody's nickname was "Rube"? Besides Hall of Fame pitchers Rube Marquard and Rube Waddell, there was also Rube Bressler. Bressler was one of Connie Mack's Athletics featured in what may be the greatest baseball book ever written.

In the 1960s, an NYU history professor named Lawrence Ritter embarked on a pilgrimage, seeking old-time baseball players—some famous, some Cooperstown inductees, others little remembered by history—for a book of remembrance called *The Glory of Their Times.* One of the chapters included an interview with Bressler.

The Bressler chapter starts with an editorial from *Baseball Magazine* in 1914: "It is, as a rule, a man's own business how he spends his money. But nevertheless we wish to call attention to the fact that many men do so in a very unwise manner. A very glaring instance of this among baseball players is the recent evil tendency to purchase automobiles.

"Put the money away, boys, where it will be safe. You don't need these automobiles. That money will look mighty good later on in life. Think it over, boys."

This op-ed was typical of the era and says much about the times. Automobiles were considered evil long before global warming. Baseball players, 60 years prior to free agency, were seen as overpaid spendthrifts, certainly not bright enough to know how to handle their own finances.

In the 1920s, the public's perception of baseball players changed for several reasons. After the 1919 Black Sox scandal, Babe Ruth

That Christy Mathewson's streak of 28⅔ scoreless innings in World Series play ended when Harry Davis knocked in "Home Run" Baker with a single in the first game of the 1911 World Series between the Giants and the A's?

upgraded the game's image, although if fans at the time knew what a personal reprobate he was, their opinion of baseball would have gone even further downhill. Ruth's charm went a long way. His way with the ladies, snappy quotes to reporters, and general amiability made him popular, and, of course, no one ever played the game like he did. In addition, many players served in World War I, which impressed the populace.

Christy Mathewson, the most admired prewar player, became a sainted figure when the mustard gas he inhaled during his army service led to ill health and then death. A writer of the era, Lester Chadwick, created a popular series called Baseball Joe, as in *Baseball Joe Saving the League, Baseball Joe in the Big League,* and the like. They were fabulous. The Baseball Joe character was based on Mathewson. The books detailed his rise from prep school to Yale, up through the minor leagues, breaking into the big leagues with the New York Giants, and then on to stardom. The names were barely changed. Rogers Hornsby, for instance, was Mornsby. Rube Marquard was Markwith. Manager John McGraw was McRae.

Rube Bressler was one of the early players who captured the imagination of the sporting public. His story is typical of the ballplayer's journey. He started out swinging a sledge hammer in a railroad shop in Flemington, Pennsylvania, where he grew up.

He pitched for the Pennsylvania Railroad Shop team out of Renovo. Earle Mack, Connie's son, toured with his All-Stars to play them. Bressler pitched against them and won. Word got to the old man, who signed the 17-year-old Bressler and sent him to Harrisburg of the Tri-State League in 1913.

By 1914 he was on Mack's staff, a starting pitcher on one of the best teams of all time—a team that won three world championships in four years. In order to get mound time, Bressler simply had to compete against the likes of Eddie Plank, Chief Bender, and Herb Pennock—all members of the Hall of Fame! Then there was "Bullet

Joe" Bush, Jack Coombs, Bob Shawkey, and Weldon Wyckoff, all top-drawer hurlers themselves.

Rube, at age 19, was 10–4 with a 1.77 earned-run average. In 1914 Bressler was just taking up space, until the A's were scheduled to face Ray Collins of Boston.

"He beat us regularly," Rube told Ritter. "Just tossed his glove on the mound and we were finished. Connie probably figured why waste a regular starter when Collins was going against us, so he threw me in there. And I won."

Two years later, he was "back in the bushes again. Couldn't win a game to save my life. Twenty-one years old and evidently all washed up."

Mack "really respected his fellow man," said Rube. "If you made a mistake, Connie never bawled you out on the bench, or in front of anybody else. He'd get you alone a few days later, and then he'd say

Rube Bressler broke onto Connie Mack's staff, but injuries curtailed his promising career. Photo courtesy of Bettmann/CORBIS.

TRIVIA

"Rube" certainly was a common nickname. Rube Bressler had a teammate named Rube. Who was it?

Answers to the trivia questions are on pages 196–198.

something like, 'Don't you think it would have been better if you'd made the play this way?'"

Bressler told Ritter that Mack did more for baseball than any other person, upholding himself as a hero to children and actually living up to it in his private life. He felt that the real reason the game's image improved was that so many young players emulated Mack to one degree or another. For this reason, Bressler said, the character of our national pastime improved.

"That '$100,000 infield'—Stuffy McInnis, Eddie Collins, Jack Barry, Frank Baker," Bressler recalled, "I don't know of any better infield ever played together. Wally Schang and Jack Lapp catching, Eddie Murphy, Amos Strunk in the outfield, and you know the pitching staff. Three future Hall of Famers, that's all.... You can't do much better than that, can you?"

According to Bressler, Eddie Collins was "the smartest player who ever lived," and "there was only one Babe Ruth. He went on the ball field like he was playing in a cow pasture, with cows for an audience. He never knew what fear or nervousness was. He played by instinct, sheer instinct. He wasn't smart, he didn't have any education, but he never made a wrong move on a baseball field."

Bressler broke in with the 1914 A's, thought to be the most experienced and veteran team of that great run. They were the best of Mack's teams until 1929. The 1914 A's lost to the weakest of all their World Series opponents: Manager George Stallings's Miracle Braves, who went from last place at the traditional July 4 break to the National League championship before knocking off Philadelphia four straight in the fall classic.

There is great similarity between the 1929 team and the 1990 Oakland team, figured to be Tony La Russa's best, ready to win a second straight World Series and establish themselves as Oakland's all-time greatest club, before losing to Cincinnati in four games.

Mack's influence apparently filtered down to the interaction between veterans and rookies. On most teams, such as John McGraw's

Giants, veterans acted toward rookies like growling dogs protecting meat. First-year players were denied their cuts in batting practice, had their bats broken, and endured hazing until they were established.

In Detroit the hazing took on a political flavor. When the Georgia-born Ty Cobb came up with a giant chip on his shoulder in 1906, "still fighting the Civil War," his northern teammates dealt with him especially harshly. When Cobb hit his stride, however, he became, "the most feared man in the history of baseball," according to Bressler.

Bressler broke into a pitching rotation led by Bender and Plank, who had each been with the team more than a decade, yet they treated him "wonderful. Just wonderful. Two of the finest guys who ever lived."

Bender, whom Mack arranged to have room with the rookie, was "one of the kindest and finest men who ever lived. See, Connie roomed a youngster with a veteran. He didn't room two youngsters together, where they could cry on each other's shoulders and commiserate with each other. ('Oh, you'll do better, dear, tomorrow.') No, sir. He had an old pitcher in there with a young one."

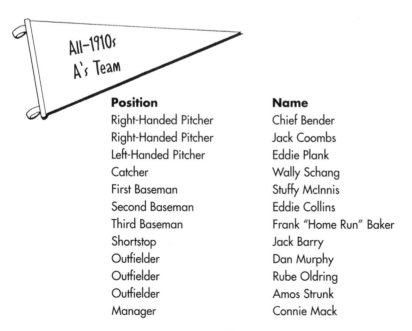

All-1910s A's Team

Position	Name
Right-Handed Pitcher	Chief Bender
Right-Handed Pitcher	Jack Coombs
Left-Handed Pitcher	Eddie Plank
Catcher	Wally Schang
First Baseman	Stuffy McInnis
Second Baseman	Eddie Collins
Third Baseman	Frank "Home Run" Baker
Shortstop	Jack Barry
Outfielder	Dan Murphy
Outfielder	Rube Oldring
Outfielder	Amos Strunk
Manager	Connie Mack

When Bressler lost a heartbreaker, 1–0, to the great Walter Johnson of Washington, Bender told Rube that he had to just forget about it and move on to the next one, that "it's a matter of record now. Forget about that game. Win the next one."

After 1914 Rube's arm went bad. Today he probably would have headed over to the Jobe-Kerlan Clinic to have laser surgery and repair a torn rotator cuff, but not so in those days. With the advent of the Federal League, which lured Bender and a few other stars, Mack lost his team. He could not pay his $100,000 infield. The team descended into the second division.

Bressler felt Philadelphia Phillies pitcher Grover Alexander was "the greatest of them all because of the conditions under which he pitched. Sixteen shutouts in 1916 pitching at Baker Bowl, where there was practically only a running track between first base and the right-field wall. Only a giant could do a thing like that."

Yankee Killers

Much changed between 1914 and 1929. World War I began in Europe in 1914. In 1917 the United States entered the war and helped win the Meuse-Argonne Offensive, giving the Allies victory in 1918. In 1919 the Chicago "Black Sox" threw the World Series against Cincinnati at the behest of gamblers.

Babe Ruth was traded to the Yankees prior to the 1920 season. To revive interest in the game after the Black Sox scandal, the ball was tightened, starting the live-ball era. Pitchers were no longer allowed to throw spitters and other doctored pitches, with the exception of a small number of hurlers identified as "spitball specialists."

Ruth went on a decade-long home-run spree, turning baseball into our national pastime and establishing his New York Yankees as the greatest team in sports. Notre Dame and Southern California popularized college football, while Red Grange did the same for the NFL. America fell in love with all sports: baseball, football, boxing, and track.

Charles Lindbergh flew across the Atlantic. The new American literary voices of a "Lost Generation"—Hemingway, Fitzgerald, Stein, Miller—captured postwar angst. The economy flourished under conservative Republican leadership, but everything crashed to a halt when the stock market collapsed on Black Monday in October 1929.

Throughout all of these years, one thing had been constant: Philadelphia A's mediocrity. Toward the late 1920s, Mack had a combination of old and young. The old included Ty Cobb, playing out his career after years in Detroit, along with former Brooklyn Dodger star

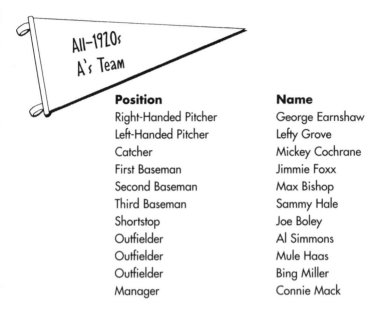

All-1920s
A's Team

Position	Name
Right-Handed Pitcher	George Earnshaw
Left-Handed Pitcher	Lefty Grove
Catcher	Mickey Cochrane
First Baseman	Jimmie Foxx
Second Baseman	Max Bishop
Third Baseman	Sammy Hale
Shortstop	Joe Boley
Outfielder	Al Simmons
Outfielder	Mule Haas
Outfielder	Bing Miller
Manager	Connie Mack

Zack Wheat, the great Tris Speaker, and the veteran Eddie Collins, making a Philadelphia curtain call.

But youth was served in pitcher Lefty Grove, first baseman Jimmie Foxx, infielders Jimmy Dykes and Max Bishop, catcher Mickey Cochrane, and outfielder Al Simmons. The 1927–28 Yankees are regarded by many to this day as the greatest team ever assembled, but Grove had their number. Their only shutout came against Lefty.

The Murderer's Row Yankees of Ruth and Lou Gehrig swept the St. Louis Cardinals in the 1928 World Series, but the A's won 98 games, finishing only two and a half back. Grove won 24 games, and Simmons hit .351. In his last year, Cobb was still outstanding, hitting .323.

At season's end, Mack finally parted with the past. Cobb retired, and Hall of Famer Speaker, who had hooked on under Mack after years with Boston and Cleveland, was sent to the minors and eventually retired.

Mack had built his team using strong scouting contacts. Cochrane came out of the Pacific Coast League, Simmons from the Milwaukee minor league club, and Grove for $100,000 from

Baltimore. "Home Run" Baker discovered the 17-year-old Foxx, who became known as "Double X" because of the two *x*'s in his name.

Mack's surprise move, pitching Howard Ehmke in the first game of the 1929 World Series versus the Chicago Cubs, had developed out of careful scouting, too. A week before the regular season ended, Mack approached Ehmke.

In a photo taken one month prior to Black Monday (the stock-market crash of 1929), future Hall of Famers (from left) Jimmie Foxx, Mickey Cochrane, and Al Simmons flex their "guns." Photo courtesy of AP/Wide World Photos.

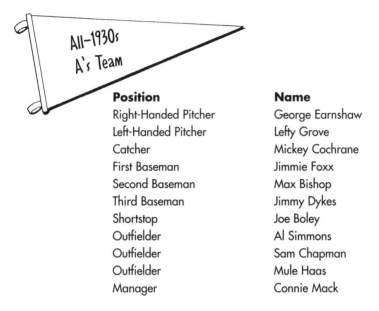

All-1930s A's Team

Position	Name
Right-Handed Pitcher	George Earnshaw
Left-Handed Pitcher	Lefty Grove
Catcher	Mickey Cochrane
First Baseman	Jimmie Foxx
Second Baseman	Max Bishop
Third Baseman	Jimmy Dykes
Shortstop	Joe Boley
Outfielder	Al Simmons
Outfielder	Sam Chapman
Outfielder	Mule Haas
Manager	Connie Mack

"Howard, you're going to pitch the first game against the Cubs for me," he told him.

"But the season won't be over for another week, or more," Ehmke replied.

"I know," said Mack. "But while we're making our last western trip, the Cubs will be playing New York and Philadelphia on their eastern swing. I want you to stay behind and scout them."

Against Cubs ace Charlie Root, Ehmke was untouchable, striking out a Series-record 13. The A's took the Series in five games. In 1930 the 102-victory A's beat the St. Louis Cardinals' Gashouse Gang in six games to capture the World Series.

The 1931 Series was an all-time classic, featuring a rematch between Philadelphia (107–45, 13½ games ahead of New York) and St. Louis (101–53). The tone was set when Pepper Martin not only managed three hits off Grove, but also stole third on Cochrane, an unthinkable feat. A few days later he did it again! Grove won the opener, 6–2, but St. Louis refused to fold. Martin hit .500 for the Series, leading the Cards to a stirring seventh-game win, with veteran spitballer Burleigh Grimes outdueling George Earnshaw in the finale, 4–2.

The fact that St. Louis is such a terrific baseball town stems in large part from the colorful Gashouse Gang of the 1930s. Dizzy Dean later joined them and in 1934 won 30 games to lead them to another world title before Stan Musial's teams of the 1940s stirred further excitement.

Hall of Famer Grove won 20 games per season for seven seasons (1927–1933), including 28 in 1930 and an unreal 31–4 mark with a 2.06 ERA in 1931. When the Depression made it impossible for Mack to maintain salaries, Grove was finally dealt to Boston in 1934, where he won 20 in 1935, finished up with 300 lifetime wins, and retired in 1941 considered to be the greatest southpaw ever.

Another Hall of Fame player, Foxx, hit 58 homers in 1932 with 169 runs batted in. Old "Double X" went to the Red Sox in 1936 and finished with 534 home runs.

Cochrane hit .331 in 1929, .357 in 1930, and .349 in 1931. Unlike Foxx and Grove, he played on winners after Mack dealt him to the 1934 American League champion Detroit Tigers. A .320 lifetime hitter, Mickey went to the Hall in 1947 and was thought to be, along with Bill Dickey of the Yankees, the greatest of all catchers until Johnny Bench, Mike Piazza, and Ivan Rodriguez came along.

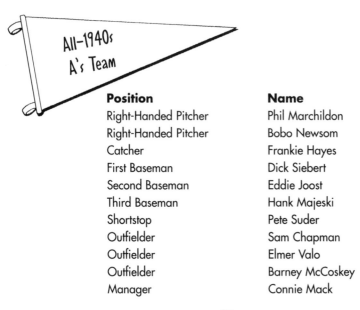

All-1940s
A's Team

Position	Name
Right-Handed Pitcher	Phil Marchildon
Right-Handed Pitcher	Bobo Newsom
Catcher	Frankie Hayes
First Baseman	Dick Siebert
Second Baseman	Eddie Joost
Third Baseman	Hank Majeski
Shortstop	Pete Suder
Outfielder	Sam Chapman
Outfielder	Elmer Valo
Outfielder	Barney McCoskey
Manager	Connie Mack

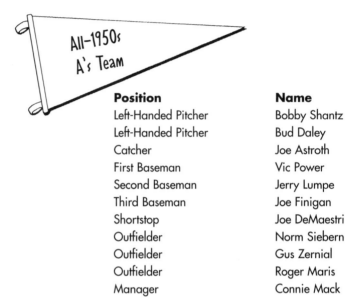

All-1950s A's Team

Position	Name
Left-Handed Pitcher	Bobby Shantz
Left-Handed Pitcher	Bud Daley
Catcher	Joe Astroth
First Baseman	Vic Power
Second Baseman	Jerry Lumpe
Third Baseman	Joe Finigan
Shortstop	Joe DeMaestri
Outfielder	Norm Siebern
Outfielder	Gus Zernial
Outfielder	Roger Maris
Manager	Connie Mack

Third baseman Jimmy Dykes hit over .300 in 1929 and 1930. The Philadelphia native was elected to Cooperstown on the strength of his defense and managerial career in Chicago.

Aloysius Harry "Bucketfoot" Simmons, also known as Al, was a throwback from Wisconsin. In 1929 he hit 34 homers with 157 RBIs and a .365 average. In 1930 he swatted 36 homers to go with 165 runs batted in and a .381 average. In 1931 he had 22 home runs, 128 RBIs, and a .390 batting average. When Simmons was traded to the White Sox, the A's lost the edge they needed against resurgent New York. Elected to the Hall of Fame in 1953, Simmons had a .334 lifetime average with 307 home runs.

Hawk

The A's history, from Rube Waddell to Reggie Jackson to Jose Canseco to Barry Zito, consists of many players who were colorful and entertaining for more than just their on-field skills. Many A's were intelligent, outspoken, and, to one degree or another, controversial.

It is unfortunate that one such player got away before adding to the team's legend. Ken "Hawk" Harrelson came up with the Kansas City A's in the mid-1960s, but was lost in a strange twist of fate to the Boston Red Sox in 1967. He became a well-known Boston personality, then a popular broadcaster with the Chicago White Sox. His name does not come up much when discussing the great, fascinating history of the A's under Charlie O. Finley, which is a shame. He would have fit in quite nicely on the Swingin' A's clubhouse of the 1970s—not to mention, they could have used his highly productive bat.

Harrelson's travails under Finley were nicely documented in Bill Libby's great 1975 book, *Charlie O. & the Angry A's.* Harrelson was called "the Hawk" because he had a nose like one.

"He was proud of it, as if it made him a modern-day Cyrano de Bergerac," wrote Libby.

As Libby pointed out, Hawk was ahead of his time, or at least part of the new times he helped mold. Baseball had always had its share of partiers, drinkers, gamblers, reprobates, womanizers, shady characters, and playboys. Babe Ruth was all of the above (well, maybe not a gambler). But the 1960s created a new dynamic among athletes. The young medium of television, greater media coverage, and a desire for greater openness led to the creation of a different, "mod" antihero, if you will.

DID YOU KNOW . . . That when Charlie O. Finley bought the A's, he burned a bus—a symbol of the "shuttle bus"—of traded A's players to the Yankees? He vowed on June 9 of his first season, "I gave the fans in Kansas City my word we would not trade with the Yankees, and my word is my bond." Six days later he traded his best pitcher, Bud Daley, to the Yankees.

The old clichés and the "secret handshake" between writers and players, in which their peccadilloes would not be reported, were on the way out. Black players became outspoken, political, even militant. Jim Bouton's *Ball Four* exposed supposed heroes as flawed men, sex freaks, pill poppers, and beer swillers.

The playboy athlete emerged, usually a guy with long hair, maybe a mustache, and the mod clothing styles worthy of a Who album. There was Bo Belinsky of the Los Angeles Angels, Derek Sanderson of the Boston Bruins, Joe Namath of the New York Jets, Dick Stuart of the Red Sox, Joe Pepitone of the Yankees, and Ken Harrelson.

"I raise my average 20 points if I know I look bitchin' out there," said Stuart, referring to the new style of uniform he wore. He was the first to eschew the old baggy pants of the 1950s for the sleeker, tighter look popularized in the game over the next years.

I Can't Wait for Tomorrow, Because I Get Better Lookin' Every Day was actually the title of "Broadway Joe" Namath's autobiography.

"You handsome son of a gun," Harrelson liked to say of himself, "don't you ever die."

Harrelson was around for a typical Finley incident that occurred in Chicago. Finley had a mule named—of course—Charlie O., and he threatened to gallop the beast onto the field in protest over some minor slight. In reality, it was just a publicity stunt. The White Sox responded with police, who were charged with keeping the animal out of the stadium. Finley fooled everybody, bringing a different mule to the party he was hosting across the street so as to lure the cops into thinking Charlie O. (the mule) was in one place when he was in another. Meanwhile, Charlie O. (the owner) sneaked Charlie O. (the mule) into the park, where he showed up on the field during a game. To accomplish this feat, Finley got Harrelson to help him.

Hawk pushed the animal out on the grass and ended up in an altercation with the mule, injuring his foot badly enough to keep him out of the lineup for three days.

Finley liked Harrelson, but they ran afoul of each other when, after a game in which Hawk's defensive skills left something to be desired, the owner found him goofing off afterward in the clubhouse, smoking a cigarette.

On another occasion, Harrelson punched an umpire in Venezuela, causing an international uproar.

And there were other incidents involving other players. After pitcher Lew Krausse was accused of firing a bullet from his hotel window at the Phillips Petroleum Building in Kansas City—presumably as a prank and not as an act of ecoterrorism—the cops were unable to pin the evidence on Krausse. But Finley took to spying on his team, allegedly using broadcaster Monte Moore as his eyes and ears, although Moore denied it.

Krausse and others reportedly got drunk and became quite "friendly" with a stewardess during a flight, causing Finley to blow his top. Relations between the owner and players soured. Although Harrelson had little to do with the "mile-high-club" incident, he did tell a reporter that Finley was "bad for baseball." That statement was enlarged to "a menace to baseball" by the time it made the TV news, causing Hawk's roommate Mike Hershberger to fall off his bed laughing.

Finley took action. He fired the Hawk.

"Kenny, I've done you a few favors," Finley told him.

"You hurt me a few times, too," said Harrelson.

"I've been good to you," Finley said. "Now I want you to write a public retraction and give it to the papers."

"Charlie, I'll be glad to retract the word *menace,* but I won't retract anything else," said Harrelson.

"That's not good enough," Finley insisted.

TRIVIA

Charlie O. Finley was not baseball's first "showman." Before Finley, what owner had a reputation for staging events and stunts to improve the fans' experience?

Answers to the trivia questions are on pages 196–198.

Finley released him. Harrelson was not yet an All-Star, but he was one of the top young prospects in the game. Finley, out of vain pride, was willing to part with him for nothing: no money, no prospects, and no player in trade or to be named later. Nada.

Finley tried to blacklist the Hawk, but he miscalculated. Finley was disliked among baseball people, who had no intention of adhering to his desires to do such a thing to a popular, talented young player. Harrelson became the first free agent in baseball history. His case opened the floodgates for the Curt Flood Supreme Court

The famed "Charlie O. the Mule" was a source of irritation to the players on owner Charlie O. Finley's teams in Kansas City and Oakland.

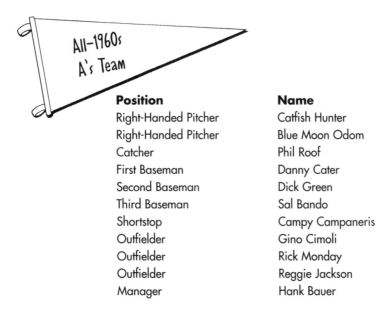

All-1960s A's Team

Position	Name
Right-Handed Pitcher	Catfish Hunter
Right-Handed Pitcher	Blue Moon Odom
Catcher	Phil Roof
First Baseman	Danny Cater
Second Baseman	Dick Green
Third Baseman	Sal Bando
Shortstop	Campy Campaneris
Outfielder	Gino Cimoli
Outfielder	Rick Monday
Outfielder	Reggie Jackson
Manager	Hank Bauer

decision, the reversal of the reserve clause, and the free-market bidding for players.

For years, high school and college stars had received huge bonuses because these prospects could freely bid on the open market. The institution of the 1965 amateur draft ended that, but the Harrelson case took it to a new level. Hawk got offers from most of Major League Baseball's teams. Hawk thought he could get $50 grand, which is what Finley would have gotten for him in a trade.

But when Paul Richards of Atlanta offered $100,000, all bets were off. Tom Yawkey of Boston, whose team had struggled for two decades and now was in a pennant race, offered Hawk $150,000. He signed with the Red Sox. In the remaining five weeks of the 1967 season, Harrelson's clutch hitting propelled Boston to the title by one game.

Harrelson was a potential superstar who never quite achieved that status, although he was *The Sporting News*'s 1968 American League Player of the Year. He later went to Cleveland but quit baseball to try his hand on the pro golf tour, ostensibly because players could wear colorful duds.

In Bill Libby's book, Harrelson said:

I have no hard feelings against Finley. I don't think he was fair to me, but he had done me a lot of favors and he wound up giving me a break. He gave me a chance to play in the World Series and make a lot of money I otherwise might not have made. I might have played on a pennant-winner with Finley's A's in Oakland. They won pennants there. I might have helped them win sooner than they did. I might have fit in with that team. Finley is a character and his is a team of characters. He's a little flaky and so am I. I guess he likes flakes. He seems to draw them to him. Once he got to Oakland he got a group of guys together that are about as flaky as guys get to be. But you can win with flakes, if they're good ballplayers. Maybe it takes flakes to live with Finley and win with him.

Charlie O.

Charles O. Finley was born and raised in the Birmingham, Alabama, area during a time that might have led some to conclude that racial prejudice was part of his makeup, but for the most part nobody really found him inclined toward those sentiments.

"Finley never showed any prejudice toward anybody," said former major leaguer and Finley employee Jimmy Piersall.

Finley, it seemed, rubbed *everybody* the wrong way, whether they were white, black, or Latino. He was a self-made man who from his earliest youth always looked for an edge. He got eggs that were discolored but not rotten from supermarkets that otherwise would have discarded them. Then he sold them at a handsome profit. He sold 12,500 subscriptions to *The Saturday Evening Post.*

As a young man, he moved to Gary, Indiana, and worked in the mills. While in Gary, he wooed the prettiest girl in town, who was not impressed. Finley moonlighted in a butcher shop to make extra money and gave her old man deals on meat, which got him on his side. She finally married him.

Finley tried to enlist in the marines when World War II hit but was declared 4-F because he had ulcers. He rose to the top as a supervisor at an ordnance plant, but when the war ended so did the need for ordnance, so he was out of work.

He became a successful insurance salesman but did not own any himself.

"I figured I'd wait until I was 40," he recalled.

He worked himself to the point of exhaustion until he came down with tuberculosis, landing him in the hospital. He was laid up

IF ONLY . . .   Ray Fosse had not been injured by Pete Rose in a
collision at the 1970 All-Star Game, Fosse may well be
considered one of baseball's great catchers.

for months and lost 100 pounds, and the majority view was that he
would die, but Finley willed himself back to health.

In the meantime, he earned no income. His illness and the
medical expenses impoverished his family. Lying in bed for months,
Finley had nothing but time to think. He came up with an insurance
plan to cover long periods of disability.

When he finally got out of the hospital, he went to his old
company and many others looking for an underwriter of his plan.
They all turned it down, so he went back to the first company that
said no, making the sale the second time around. Then he sold group
policies to the American Medical Association and the American
College of Surgeons. It was revolutionary: group insurance, covering
unforeseen disabilities, often offered by employers instead of strictly
as individual accounts. It turned him into a millionaire.

Finley used his money to buy the Kansas City A's prior to the
1961 season. The A's were considered a "Yankee farm club" that sold
its best players to New York just when they were getting good. In
seven seasons in Kansas City, the A's were mediocre. Finley was
eccentric and frugal above and beyond previous baseball concep-
tions of frugality. It earned him little success and less goodwill. After
the 1967 season, Finley just up and moved the A's from Kansas City
to Oakland. Finley was now Oakland's problem.

But despite a lack of success on the field in Kansas City, Finley
brought to Oakland the seeds of greatness. Because he was so cheap,
he paid his scouts next to nothing, firing most of them and assuming
the role himself. He had played American Legion, then some adult
semipro ball; that was the extent of his baseball experience.

Finley somehow found talent on the highways and byways of
rural America. In the 1960s, prior to the free-agent draft, there was
still undiscovered stardom waiting to be found.

Jim Hunter was a North Carolina farm boy, a promising pitcher
who lost part of his toe in a hunting accident, scaring off the scouts

and their big bonuses. Finley signed him for less. When Finley found out that after running away from home in his boyhood Hunter went fishing and returned home with a mess of catfish as a peace offering, he nicknamed him "Catfish."

John Odom was poor and black, from the Deep South. Finley, a white Southerner, charmed his mom and signed him, too. His nickname was "Moon" because his face was round. Under Finley it became "Blue Moon."

Then Finley noticed that the colleges were playing terrific baseball. He raided the roster of the 1965–66 Arizona State Sun Devils, winners of the '65 College World Series, drafting Rick Monday, Sal Bando, and Reggie Jackson, who went from Tempe, briefly to Kansas City in the Athletics' last days there, and then on to Oakland.

Hard-nosed manager Dick Williams (right) met his match in Charlie O. Finley.

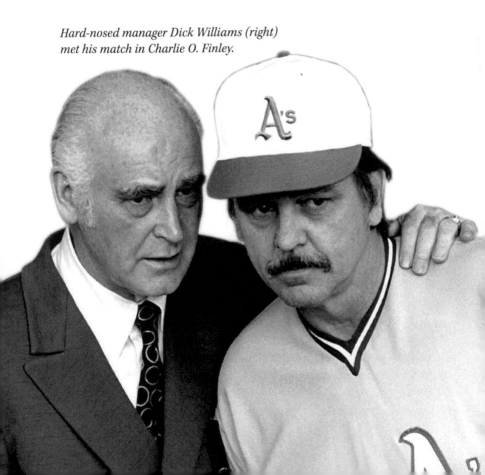

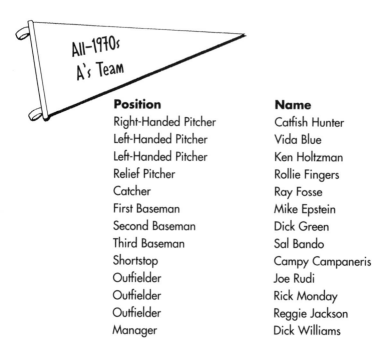

All-1970s
A's Team

Position	Name
Right-Handed Pitcher	Catfish Hunter
Left-Handed Pitcher	Vida Blue
Left-Handed Pitcher	Ken Holtzman
Relief Pitcher	Rollie Fingers
Catcher	Ray Fosse
First Baseman	Mike Epstein
Second Baseman	Dick Green
Third Baseman	Sal Bando
Shortstop	Campy Campaneris
Outfielder	Joe Rudi
Outfielder	Rick Monday
Outfielder	Reggie Jackson
Manager	Dick Williams

In Oakland, the nicknames kept on comin', all courtesy of Charlie O. Vida Blue was "True" Blue according to Finley, who offered Blue a bonus to officially change his name. There was "Sugar Bear" Daniels, a teenage pitcher who never made it, and pinch runner Allan "the Panamanian Express" Lewis.

Despite the nicknames and gimmicks, or possibly because of them, no one respected Finley. He was viewed not as a serious baseball man but as a showman. Finley had deserted Kansas City, a growing market baseball was determined to succeed in and eventually would with the expansion Royals. In the Bay Area, he was an interloper, cutting into the Giants' attendance when the game could ill afford a drop-off in fan base.

His do-it-yourself scouting system was thought to be a joke. Then there were the uniforms. Kelly green and gold with white shoes. A mechanical rabbit to feed balls to the home-plate umpire. A mule nicknamed "Charlie O." relieving itself all over the field, the hallways, and God knows where else. Everything was done on the cheap, including players' salaries, travel, and stadium upkeep.

The Bay Area did not welcome him. Attendance was never good. Finley was an absentee owner, calling the shots by phone from the Indiana suburbs outside of Chicago, and the threat of his moving or selling the team always hung in the air. He was considered a clown, a renegade. His ideas were blasphemous: night World Series and All-Star Games, designated hitters, designated pinch runners, orange baseballs, and three balls for a walk, just to name a few.

The baseball establishment could not stand him. Commissioner Bowie Kuhn despised him. Finley and his A's were the opposite of the classy, traditional franchises in Los Angeles and New York. Finley showed no loyalty to anybody, firing managers every year, and engendered no loyalty in return. It was all business.

But a funny thing happened along the way. Finley was as right as rain. The funky-named country boys and college kids he scouted and signed, often against conventional wisdom, consistently panned out. He may have been lucky once or twice, but his signings, trades, and intuition were so dead-on good, time after time over so many years, that like him or hate him Charles Finley must be considered a baseball genius. Pure and simple.

Without anyone taking notice, Finley's A's went from downright bad in Kansas City to a team of great youth and hope for the future in Oakland. The A's broke the .500 mark in their first year in Oakland, then contended with Minnesota in 1969 and 1970 with 88 and 89 wins, respectively.

Finley's bad press and poor public relations resulted in lousy attendance despite one of the most exciting young teams in the game. The A's never drew, no matter how spectacular they played. The reason was Finley's public demeanor.

Young player after young player, many scouted by Finley personally, was signed and performed beautifully in the A's minor league system. In the late 1960s and early '70s, Rollie Fingers, Chuck Dobson, Vida Blue, Gene Tenace, Bert Campaneris, Sal Bando, Joe Rudi, and Reggie Jackson blossomed into genuine stars. Then Finley would

TRIVIA

Aside from the A's, what other professional sports franchises were owned by Charlie O. Finley?

Answers to the trivia questions are on pages 196–198.

orchestrate unbelievable trades, à la Billy Beane. He would seemingly bamboozle hardened baseball men, lifting washed-up veterans and untested rookies who, once in Oakland, found themselves playing key roles on winning teams.

Mike Epstein and Darold Knowles came over from the Washington Senators. Ken Holtzman was obtained for Rick Monday, one of the best trades ever. Felipe and Matty Alou were productive hitters in Oakland.

Finley fired managers and hired retreads who under his employ were (or should be) Hall of Famers. Dick Williams was run out of Boston and led Oakland to two straight world championships. Alvin Dark was fired by half of baseball, including Finley in the 1960s, but managed the 1974 A's to a five-game drubbing of a Dodgers team thought to be superior in the World Series.

Everybody was supposed to be better than Finley's A's, until Finley's A's left 'em in the dust. The Big Red Machine. The Oriole dynasty. The hallowed Dodgers—with all their money, the tradition and palm-treed, sun-splashed shrine of a stadium—came into the "mausoleum," which is what Sal Bando called the unkempt Oakland Coliseum, only to leave not knowing what hit 'em.

Finley's ideas were almost all adopted for better (night All-Star and postseason games) or for worse, depending on your perspective (designated hitter), with a few never making the cut (orange balls, designated runners, three-ball walks).

Finley's "general manager" in his last years was a teenage black rapper later known as MC Hammer, then just Hammer. In the end, Finley, the man of new ideas, the innovator, succumbed to newer, really bad ideas: free agency and unionization. He almost drove baseball out of Oakland, left in ignominy, divorced his wife, and had few loyal friends—most that speak of him do so without much kindness in their hearts. But everybody respected his baseball genius and ability to build a champion almost by himself. He remains one of the truly unique characters in the game's history. Some might compare him to George Steinbrenner, in that they are both gruff and demanding, but Steinbrenner does not possess one iota of Finley's acumen for judging talent.

They Weren't That Wild about Harry

The A's fooled around with different radio stations and announcers their first few years in Oakland. Monte Moore was always around, but he did not seem to have the gravitas to carry a broadcast the way Russ Hodges and Lon Simmons, who did Giants games, did.

In 1970 Finley brought in a whale. A whale, in legal or sales terms—some call them rainmakers—is someone with a big name, a big past, and enough reputation to carry the firm, the company, the team to greater heights, that is, increase ticket sales and fan base and just generally bring in more moola.

Before Harry Caray was a legend in Chicago he was a legend in St. Louis, where he was fired as the Cardinals announcer after the 1969 season. It seems that Harry fell from grace because he was playing fast and loose with a young woman who had married into the August A. Busch clan. Caray never answered the tawdry allegations. Still others rumored (unconfirmed) that the woman was actually Busch's wife.

"I'd rather have people believing the rumor and have my middle-aged ego inflated than deny it and keep my job," was Caray's nondenial denial.

It was always something with Harry.

"My car stalled outside the Chase Park Plaza Hotel in St. Louis, where I used to spend a lot of time," he once recalled. "I was sitting there, about 4:00 in the morning, cursing my bad luck, when these two guys came up to me. Each of them stuck a gun in my ribs. Hoo boy! Then one of them said, 'Hey, Harry. It's you, isn't it? What're you doing out this late? Are you one of us?' I'd been a broadcaster in St. Louis for 25 years, you know, so I was pretty well known there. Well, this guy put his gun away, and we just stood there jawing about baseball. They forgot they were mugging me. We were all just fans. I signed a couple of autographs, and they took off without taking a nickel."

A guy like this is either going to get along great with Charlie O. Finley or get into a brawl with him. Finley bet, after Caray's postdalliance firing in St. Louis, that they would get along great.

In 1970 baseball fans on the West Coast were still getting their feet wet. They knew Vin Scully down in L.A., and of course Hodges had shouted, "The Giants win the pennant! The Giants win the pennant! The Giants win the pennant!" after Bobby Thomson's 1951 "shot heard 'round the world." Hodges's partner, Simmons, was more made for San Francisco: easygoing, like a soft ocean breeze. Bill King of the Raiders and Warriors was the voice of the East Bay—like Simmons, a unique Bay Area personality with his love of the opera, Heifetz references, and overall erudition.

But A's fans were trying to get a frame of reference for their team, a very important part of fan development. Moore was from Oklahoma. People tried to understand what Finley was attempting to convey. With his mule on the field before games and a Dixieland jazz troupe playing the stands during the contests, was he trying to

TOP 10

Oakland A's Announcers

1. Bill King
2. Lon Simmons
3. Ken Korach
4. Ray Fosse
5. Greg Papa
6. Monte Moore
7. Harry Caray
8. Red Rush
9. Bob Elston
10. Jimmy Piersall

Harry Caray announces his last game for the Cardinals. After St. Louis fired him, he was exiled to Oakland, where Charlie O. Finley also fired him. Photo courtesy of AP/Wide World Photos.

make Oakland the Midwest of the West? They needed someone else. Caray was available, so Finley took a chance on him.

When spring training got under way, the A's games were on the air, a fairly new concept. Most teams did not broadcast exhibitions, or if they did just weekend games. But that *voice!*

In those days, before cable TV, ESPN, the Internet, and the nationalization of sports we see today, a fan on the West Coast may very well not know much, or anything, about somebody like Harry Caray, even though he had been the booming voice of Cardinals baseball on KMOX for years. Finley, the midwestern businessman, had been listening to him for years. Showman Charlie thought Caray's bombastic style would make him the perfect ringmaster of Finley's kelly green–and–gold circus.

But again, that *voice!* Harry lisped, he sounded drunk—he often was—he was way too loud, and in the end he insulted Mr. Finley, the ultimate no-no.

Rick Monday, who played for the Cubs, was on the Oakland A's the one year (1970) that Harry was an announcer for Finley.

"One day we were waiting in the bus outside the ballpark," Monday recalled. "Somebody said the only one we were waiting for was Harry. One of the players got impatient and said, 'Oh, Harry told me to say he's taking a cab.' So the bus takes off without him, and Harry comes out, no bus. He buried that guy on the air, just buried him. Later he tipped a skycap at the airport 100 bucks to have the guy's bags shipped to Tokyo."

Harry could restore his affections for a player just as easily. These shifts in attitude did not always sit well with players, who prefer to think of announcers as part of the team. The players complained to Charlie O. about Harry. The refined Bay Area listening audience did not relate. Harry probably got drunk and made a pass at Finley's wife...or daughter. In any case, he was gone by 1971.

Caray's story, of course, does not end there. He went to Chicago, where he broadcast White Sox games. Harry's relations with former White Sox manager Chuck Tanner were frequently strained. Tanner disapproved of Harry's on-air jabs and was particularly chafed at his popularity with the fans. Eventually, Harry found his way to the place he would call home until the end: Wrigley Field and the Cubs.

Harry was Midwest all the way. Maybe over time the California audience would have come to appreciate him, but no Chicago summer was complete without Harry, banana daiquiri in hand, making his early-morning rounds in the drinking quarter where State and Rush streets converge. Revelers would follow him, chanting his name. Cabdrivers would stall traffic to hail him. Barflies would call, "Hey, Harry," as if he were their best friend. Harry's response was usually an engaging and familiar "Hiya, sweetheart" for the ladies and "Whaddaya say, pal" for the dudes. "You're the greatest." "Hey, Harry, say hello to the people of the world." It was like Norm on *Cheers,* only the bar was the whole city of Chicago, north and south sides. Prostitutes would stop him for autographs.

TRIVIA

The first A's game in Oakland drew a capacity crowd of more than 50,000 fans. What was the attendance the next night?

Answers to the trivia questions are on pages 196–198.

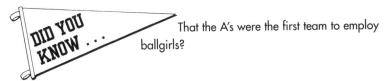

That the A's were the first team to employ ballgirls?

Harry would call players on the phone, not leaving the message that "Harry called," but rather giving the name of the ballclub owner so as to assure a return call. The biggest sin a player could commit, in Harry's eyes, was to disparage the fans. This belief made Harry popular with fans, not always with players.

Harry was married numerous times. His real wife was baseball. His tagline was "Ho-ly Cow." He sang "Take Me Out to the Ball Game" during the seventh-inning stretch. He would lean out of the broadcast booth to communicate with fans. Bill Veeck, the former White Sox announcer, thought Harry fit in with his fans' raucous style (remember "Disco Demolition Night"?) and that he would not fit in with the Cubs. Of course, when Harry made the switch from Comiskey to Wrigley, he was deified by the Cubbie faithful. It seems that he was made to order for Chicago's entertaining but usually unsuccessful teams.

Harry was, to be honest, the most unprepared announcer in the game, bungling names and facts without a care in the world. Still, there is no doubt that Harry was responsible for raising attendance on the north and south sides, which is what really counts. On Saturdays, he did his broadcast from among the "bleacher bums," beer in hand. Harry represented something the game no longer has. The new corporate owners would no more tolerate his antics than they would keep a low-performing stock in their portfolios.

Slurring his words on air, Harry would say, "Thammy Thotha's gonna be a thuperthtar." Outside of Ernie Banks and Michael Jordan, Harry Caray will live on as one of the most popular sports figures in Chicago history, but he is a small part of Oakland baseball history, too.

Williams Would Be in the Hall if He'd Been in New York

It was April 1971. The Oakland A's, favored to win the American League West under new manager Dick Williams, were off to a bad start. Vida Blue was rocked by Washington, 8–0, in the Presidential Opener. On a raw, cold day at the Oakland Coliseum, Chicago swept the A's in a doubleheader. The team hit the road again and continued to flounder. After losing 10–5 to Kansas City on a Sunday, the club found itself bouncing through a thunder-and-lightning-filled sky on the way to Milwaukee.

Williams fortified himself throughout the trip with scotch, in reaction to his team's 2–4 record as much as to the bumpy flight. By the time the plane touched down at Billy Mitchell Field, he was in a nasty mood. The players, relieved to be on terra firma, were in jovial spirits as they boarded the bus for the Pfister Hotel. As the bus rolled through the streets, traveling secretary Tom Corwin whispered to Williams that somebody had pilfered a battery-powered bullhorn, part of the plane's emergency equipment.

Williams stood up, walked about a quarter of the way to the back of the bus, and faced the players.

"Gentlemen," he began, "some of you think you can be pricks. But I've got news for you; I can be the biggest prick of all. I've been mild up to now."

Williams then told his new team that there would be no more drinking on flights and that if they knew what was good for them, players would stay in their rooms the entire trip, except to come to the ballpark. The bullhorn was produced.

Rollie Fingers threw a four-hit shutout the next afternoon (yes, Rollie Fingers). Vida Blue tossed a two-hitter the next day, and Oakland went on to win 101 games and the division crown.

There are many different schools of thought. Some managers talk tough but cannot or will not back it up. Dick Williams was old school. He talked tough, and he backed it up.

In 2001 the Veterans Committee of the Baseball Hall of Fame inducted ex-Pirate infielder Bill Mazeroski and old-time Negro Leaguer Hilton Smith into Cooperstown, but Williams did not make the grade. Williams was asked his opinion on the subject. Most guys reach into the Universal Cliché Handbook when confronted by such questions: "If that's God's plan, then so be it," or "I don't worry about things beyond my control."

"I absolutely deserve to be in there," was Williams's answer.

The fact is, Williams was a first-class baseball man. He came out of Fremont High School in Los Angeles, a place that has produced more major leaguers than any high school in the country. Something that produces tough-as-nails managers must have been running through the water fountains at Fremont, because Gene Mauch came out of there, too. Sparky Anderson prepped a few blocks away at Dorsey.

TOP 10

All-Time A's Managers

1. Connie Mack
2. Dick Williams
3. Tony La Russa
4. Alvin Dark
5. Art Howe
6. Ken Macha
7. Billy Martin
8. Hank Bauer
9. John McNamara
10. Bobby Winkles

Williams was not a great ballplayer, but like some other feisty Californians who would manage—Mauch and Billy Martin come to mind—he was a natural.

In 1966 he managed Boston's Triple A club to a championship, and the next year he found himself in charge of a Red Sox team described as a "country club." The team's star, Carl Yastrzemski, was an overpaid, underperforming outfielder. Williams lit a fire under Yaz, who won the Triple Crown and led Boston to within one game of the world championship.

Unfortunately, Williams could not get along with Red Sox owner Tom Yawkey, one of the nicest guys in sports, and was fired a couple of years later. In 1971 Williams was hired by the Anti-Nice. His name was Charles O. Finley.

Amazingly, these two fireballs were right for each other, for a while. Finley would call Williams at all hours of the day and night—at the hotel, at the park, at his home while barbecuing on an off

From left, Reggie Jackson, Dick Williams, and Catfish Hunter had one thing in common: they did not like Charlie O. Finley.

By the NUMBERS **288-190**—Dick Williams's managerial record in Oakland.

Year	Won	Lost
1971	101	60
1972	93	62
1973	94	68

day—to order lineup changes, roster maneuvers, and different strategy.

Finley knew baseball and had a knack for scouting talent. The A's were loaded, and in 1972 and 1973 the club won world championships. At that point, Williams announced that he could no longer stand Finley, so he left to go to work for the loveable George Steinbrenner, who was in his post-illegal-contributions-to–Richard Nixon period. Williams never actually did manage under Steinbrenner, who established a pattern of firing managers that would continue up until the Joe Torre era.

Williams did return to California to lead the San Diego Padres to the Series in 1984 and had a 1,571–1,451 career record. One might speculate that had Williams been more personable with members of the press, as Sparky Anderson was, he might be in the Hall of Fame. He and Bill McKechnie are the only managers to take three teams to the fall classic.

With all due respect to the lovable Bill Rigney, the apostle Alvin Dark, the genius Tony La Russa, and the exalted Dusty Baker, Williams may just be the best manager in Bay Area history. Hall of Fame? If his accomplishments had come in New York rather than on the West Coast, he would have been in there a long time ago.

Cap'n Sal

Dick Williams called him "Mr. Dependable," the "old pro who keeps this team together."

"The only reason [Joe] Rudi and me and a few others seem so steady is that the rest of these guys are stark raving crazy," was "Cap'n Sal" Bando's assessment of his place on the angry A's of the early 1970s.

"On this club, if you go to sleep at night and wake up in the morning, you're considered strange," he continued. "Anyone who isn't arguing with Finley or throwing a punch at a teammate isn't with it. We all love each other. We just show our feelings in strange ways. We're together in wanting to win. Let's just say we have spirit."

That "spirit" manifested itself in funny ways, like the time outfielders Billy North and Reggie Jackson got into a clubhouse fight over a mutual girlfriend or the time Vida Blue and John Odom scrapped, just before Odom and Blue teamed up to win the deciding game of the 1972 American League championship series at Detroit.

Bando grew up in Cleveland in a close-knit Italian American family. He turned down offers to play quarterback in college to concentrate on baseball. This led him to Bobby Winkles and Arizona State, the first great A's "farm club" of the Finley dynasty. Future Oakland teammates included Rick Monday and Jackson. Finley signed Bando for $30,000.

Bando was part of the great youth wave that moved through the system. He came up through Modesto and Vancouver, then played 11 games in the big leagues in 1966. Some of his prominent teammates came up late in the 1967 season at Kansas City. Under Manager Bob Kennedy at Oakland in 1968, they all made the major

In an enormous upset, the colorful A's celebrate victory over Cincinnati in the 1972 World Series. From left are Sal Bando, Rollie Fingers, and Dave Duncan.

league roster in spring training. Bando had the third-base job, and he would never relinquish it.

He was built like a bowling ball, with a barrel chest and the visage of Paulie from the Rocky series. Hard shots down the third-base line were not skillfully scooped up by Bando the way they were by Baltimore's Brooks Robinson or New York's Graig Nettles. Often, Bando would just place his chest in front of the ball, let it bounce to the ground, pick it up, then throw the man out at first base. He practiced it that way in pregame drills. How black-and-blue he was could not be determined, because he had a Sherwood Forest of hair on his chest.

"I wasn't as spectacular as some others, so I didn't get the money some did," said Bando. He claimed he was not "as spectacular as Reggie Jackson or a Vida Blue, so I don't get their kind of money or get their sort of publicity."

Bando had a solid season in 1968 and developed into a bona fide star in 1969. He played in all 162 games in both of his first two full seasons (1968 and 1969), hitting 31 homers with 113 RBIs in '69. That turned out to be his best year, but he was always good for around 25 homers and 90 runs batted in. He rarely got hurt and played through it if he was.

Bando was often in the hunt for the American League Most Valuable Player award but lost out to teammates Blue (1971) and Jackson (1973). He was a total clutch hitter. With no one on base in the first inning, Bando was likely to flail and miss, looking over-matched by some mound ace. Then along came the eighth inning, two men on, and the game tied. *Boom!* Double off the right-center-field fence.

He was key in numerous Oakland postseason victories. In the years after Robinson declined, and before Nettles emerged as a star with the Yankees, Bando was the American League's third-base starter in the All-Star Game.

Bando had 32 doubles to lead the league in 1973, when he hit 29 home runs and drove in 98. The next season he drove in 103. He was not a .300 hitter, and his overall statistics often belied his consistency. His postseason record does not impress on the surface, except that his many key hits (the bases-clearing double being his specialty) came at just the right time. The A's of 1971 through 1975 (five consecutive division titles) were truly a team. It is not an exaggeration to say that despite the star turns of Jackson, Catfish Hunter, and others, the loss of any of their key players would have been enough to deny them any of their three World Series wins. This applies to Bando in a big way. Had Bando not been a fixture at third

TRIVIA

The 1965 Arizona State Sun Devils were considered to be the greatest college baseball team up until that time. Who were some of the Sun Devils who went on to the major leagues?

Answers to the trivia questions are on pages 196–198.

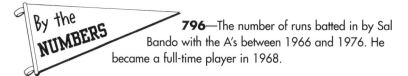

By the NUMBERS **796**—The number of runs batted in by Sal Bando with the A's between 1966 and 1976. He became a full-time player in 1968.

base from 1972 to 1974, the A's would not have won any of those championships! Even the 1972 A's won the World Series without Jackson. Pitching and ground-ball defense were the club's cornerstones. If anybody were to ask Jackson, Ray Fosse, or any of Bando's teammates, they would agree with this analysis.

"I don't stir up storms," Bando said in Bill Libby's *Charlie O. and the Angry A's.* "It's stormy enough around here without adding to it. I got a job to do. I do it. The other guys get the glamour."

While Jackson was outspoken in his denunciations of the cheapskate Finley, the poor maintenance of the Coliseum, and the love lives of teammates, Bando maintained silence—most of the time. Eventually he could not hold it in any longer, calling the Coliseum a mausoleum and stating that new manager Alvin Dark (who replaced Williams in 1974) "couldn't manage a meat market." He apologized to Dark.

The difference between the A's and every other team was that these kinds of internal animosities destroyed most clubs, but in Oakland they just rolled off the team's back. Whether Dark could manage a meat market or not, he did well enough in 1974 to lead Oakland to another World Series title.

The A's kept it together, sort of, through the 1976 season. Bando hit 27 homers that year, but it was the last hurrah for him and his team. Hunter had left for free agency prior to the 1975 season, and his departure was just enough to prevent the team from beating Boston in the playoffs and defending a fourth world championship. By 1976 Jackson was in Baltimore. Oakland still had talent—Blue, Joe Rudi, Rollie Fingers, Bando—but it was not enough. George Brett and Kansas City edged them out for the American League West title. After that, it was "Katy bar the door"—a wave of free-agent departures and trades in which Finley unloaded salary in return for cash. Attendance, never a strong point in Oakland, was abysmal.

Jackson, who remained a star in New York and Anaheim until the 1980s, always said if the team had stayed together they would

DID YOU KNOW . . . That after leaving Oakland, Sal Bando played for Milwaukee and then became the Brewers' general manager? Phil Garner, a former Athletic, went to the Brewers, too, and through the Bando connection started his managerial career there.

have won championships for the rest of the decade. Some of the departed A's—Fingers, Hunter, and Blue in particular—were superstars with other teams, but others trailed off. Bando was one of them. After he left for Milwaukee his records never approached his Oakland marks. The same was true of Gene Tenace, Rudi, and Ken Holtzman. It is tantalizing, however, to consider what kind of team Oakland might have had if the veteran nucleus was still around when Rickey Henderson, Mike Norris, and the young stars of the late 1970s emerged.

Jax

In his great book *October 1964*, David Halberstam paints a portrait of the 1964 Cardinals-Yankees World Series, using baseball as a metaphor for a changing America.

The Cardinals played National League baseball, which meant they went for the extra base, the stolen base, made things happen. They were, in Halberstam's view, the baseball version of the winning Democrats of that year.

The Yankees had few black players, and those they employed, such as Elston Howard, were strictly "organization men." The Yankees were the pinstriped, Wall Street country clubbers of the losing 1964 GOP.

The rest of the American League was slow to pick up on the new themes, preferring to emulate the Yankees even though they did not have the resources to win using those methods. But after 1964, New York faltered, leaving an opening for the rest of the league. A host of candidates—the Twins, Red Sox, and Tigers—vied for the nomination but could not attain a "mandate." Just as the Republicans regained power and established dominance in the succeeding years, in the aftermath of the fall of the Yankee Empire, so too did the Yanks and their league make a comeback.

During the 12-year period in which the Yankees were exiled to the baseball version of Elba, two teams—the Baltimore Orioles and the Oakland A's—emerged as contenders for the presidency, with Oakland winning the election via three straight world championships from 1972 to 1974.

The head of the ticket on those teams was Reggie Jackson. He straddled an economic dividing line in baseball. Jackson was not the first free agent, but his signing with the Yankees before the 1977 season had the greatest impact. He was of that class of athlete that made enough money to practically call his own shots, rising above the politics of traditional owner-player and manager-player relationships. The fireworks that came out of this paradigm shift, the verbal battles, the chess matches, and even, sometimes, the physical

The classic swing of Reggie Jackson, one of the game's greatest sluggers.

GOOD THING . . . Reggie Jackson dated a Mexican American girl with light skin at ASU or else he might have played his entire career with the Mets. Considered the best amateur prospect of the 1966 draft, Jackson was told the Mets were picking Steve Chilcott instead of him because Jackson "dated a white girl." The A's picked Jackson with the second choice. Chilcott never made the majors.

altercations between Jackson and his two principal owners—Charlie O. Finley and later George Steinbrenner—and Yankees manager Billy Martin, made for headlines that negated the blurry line between sports and entertainment.

Jackson was pure entertainment. Compared to the steroid era of the 1990s, his records pale somewhat, but based on what now seems apparent about Barry Bonds, Mark McGwire, Sammy Sosa, and many others, Jackson and players such as Willie Mays, Hank Aaron, Babe Ruth, Ted Williams, Mickey Mantle, Ken Griffey Jr., and Frank Thomas, just to name a few, can reclaim much of their lost stature.

Jackson was the essence of a winner, which is not the same as a team player, but when it comes to rings and putting money in his teammates' pockets, it is the highest of accolades. "Mr. October" was a clutch hitter in big games like no player before or since, and with all due respect this includes stalwarts like Ruth, Mantle, and...the list is that short!

When it comes to being a "money player," Aaron, Mays, Bonds, and Williams are not in Jackson's league. A handful of pitchers such as Christy Mathewson, Whitey Ford, Sandy Koufax, Bob Gibson, and Oakland teammate Jim "Catfish" Hunter were to their positions what Reggie was to his. Perhaps Michael Jordan and Jerry West in basketball and Joe Montana and Johnny Unitas in football are in this pantheon. Perhaps.

Reggie grew up in a broken home that split his youth between middle-class Philadelphia, where his father was a successful businessman, and the Baltimore projects. Reggie starred in baseball and football. His Adonis physique was natural, not just from the absence of steroids but mainly without the use of weights, at least by modern training standards. He went to Arizona State University, where he played for two legends: the grandfatherly

Bobby Winkles in baseball and the disciplinarian Frank Kush in football.

Reggie played on the 1965 ASU freshman team. The varsity won the national championship. In 1966 Reggie was an All-American and *The Sporting News*'s Player of the Year. The ASU program formed the basis of the A's champions. Jackson, Rick Monday, and Sal Bando played together at ASU and in Oakland. Even Winkles would one day be an Oakland manager.

Jackson was the second player chosen in the 1966 free-agent draft. He was sent to Birmingham, Alabama, ground zero of the 1960s civil rights struggle, and he would encounter racist remarks and handle them in his own way. Charlie O. Finley was from Birmingham. The story varies. One says that one night he was in town entertaining Alabama football coach Paul "Bear" Bryant at a Birmingham game.

The other version is that Bear was at a game because his son, Paul Jr., was the club's general manager. Whether Finley was with Bryant and invited him into the A's clubhouse or Bryant came into the clubhouse at the invitation of his son, what Bear saw there was the shirtless, muscled Jackson, to whom he was introduced. Bryant took one look at the former Sun Devil football star with the intelligent smile. Jackson quietly shook his hand and said that he had heard a lot about Bryant.

"Bryant smiled, looked away from me over to his son, and said very matter-of-factly, 'Now this is the kind of n—— boy I need to start my football program,'" said Jackson.

Jackson, had his own understanding of the context of the meeting.

"I knew he didn't mean any harm with those words," wrote Jackson in his 1984 autobiography, *Reggie*. "This was the best he could do, his way of paying me a compliment. He was drawing on his own experience, his own life, and trying to be nice."

"Yessir," added Bear, "if I could just have one like you, I could get it done real easy at school."

There are many who dispute Bryant's use of the term *n——*. Many blacks who played or coached for him insist he never talked like that. Either way, the meeting foretold unfolding events. Four

TOP 10

All-Time Home Run List

1.	Hank Aaron	755
2.	*Barry Bonds	734
3.	Babe Ruth	714
4.	Willie Mays	660
5.	*Sammy Sosa	588
6.	Frank Robinson	586
7.	*Mark McGwire	583
8.	Harmon Killebrew	573
9.	*Rafael Palmeiro	569
10.	Reggie Jackson	563

*Player accused of steroid use.

years later, after Southern California thumped Alabama at Legion Field, Bryant integrated his program. Later evidence uncovered the fact that he and USC coach John McKay had been planning the best way to effectuate this change even before Bryant's meeting with Jackson.

After hitting 47 home runs in 1969, Jackson warred with the miserly Finley over his contract. The animosity was hot and heavy throughout his disappointing 1970 season. In Chicago Jackson had to be restrained from going after the owner in the stands during a game.

By 1971 a truce was in place, and with it came Oakland glory. Jackson powered 32 home runs to lead the A's to the division title. In an era dominated by pitching, Jackson's stats were not Bonds-like, but his winning records were superior. He hit 25 homers in 1972 to lead Oakland to the American League title. Baltimore finally gave way to the newcomers from the West Coast.

In the playoffs, Jackson's clutch steal of home on a first-and-third situational play barely gave the A's a Game 5, 2–1 win over Detroit but cost the team their best player for the World Series with Cincinnati. Jackson badly tore his hamstring and had to watch the Series in street clothes and on crutches.

In one of the greatest examples of good pitching beating good hitting this side of Sandy Koufax and Don Drysdale, Oakland prevailed

DID YOU KNOW ... That Reggie Jackson went to Arizona State to play football but tried out for the baseball team to win a bet and also to avoid Coach Frank Kush's rigorous spring football practices? After hitting several balls 430 feet over the center-field fence at Sun Devil Field, Reggie asked Coach Bobby Winkles if he had made the team, to which Winkles replied, "I think we could find a place for you."

in seven games. The next year Jackson was the league MVP, carrying the team on his shoulders over Baltimore and then the Tom Seaver–Jon Matlack–Jerry Koosman Mets in the Series.

But Jackson's financial squabbles with Finley never ended, and in 1976 he was traded to Baltimore. In 1977 he signed a huge free-agent contract with the Yankees, entering the carnival atmosphere of New York just as the Yankees were emerging from a 12-year (by Yankees standards) slump. His three homers in Game 6 and five overall powered New York to a win over the Dodgers in the 1977 World Series. He led New York again in a win over Los Angeles in 1978 and in 1982 starred on the California Angels' West Division champions.

Reggie hit more than 500 homers and earned five rings. In 1973 and 1977, particularly, he came through on the biggest of all stages in the most spectacular of manners. He is a Hall of Famer and a true legend whose personality and ego match his talent.

Jackson has straddled the historical line between being an Oakland Athletic and a Yankee, both of whom claim him jealously.

"If the A's had been kept together," said Jackson, "we'd have kept winning titles into the 1980s." Because the 1980s were years in which the Yankees were winning, this statement seems to indicate that Jackson felt the best teams he ever played for were in Oakland.

The First "Louisiana Lightning"

Before Ron Guidry, the diminutive Cajun dubbed "Louisiana Lightning" when he won 25 games for the 1978 Yankees, there was Vida Blue. Blue hailed from Mansfield, Louisiana, a poor black kid raised by a single mother in an all-too-familiar social scenario.

Baseball attendance dropped in the 1960s and 1970s, for various reasons. The Vietnam War, antiwar protests (particularly in the A's backyard of Berkeley), and a sexualized society more enamored by the seductive violence of pro football drew people away from the slow-moving traditions of the diamond game.

The Bay Area failed to support either of its baseball teams. The market, at least at that time, probably was only big enough to support the Giants, so the emergence of the A's was part of the reason for the lack of support. However, considering how great the A's were (while the Giants were a picture of mediocrity for the most part), it is hard to believe Oakland could not draw better. Four hundred miles to the south, the Los Angeles Dodgers were wildly successful. The contrast between the "Dodger way" and what was going on by San Francisco Bay was stunning.

Charlie O. Finley deserves credit for his innovations and many other things, but there is no avoiding the fact that his lack of popularity drove the attendance woes of the A's. Of all the attractions on those teams, one man stands out.

Reggie Jackson was their star. Catfish Hunter was their ace. But Vida Blue was their biggest drawing card. When this author was a kid, I approached Vida for an autograph and found him engaging.

"If I had to do it all over again," he told me, "I'd have been the first black quarterback at Notre Dame."

TRIVIA

Vida Blue threw one no-hitter in his career. When did he throw it and against whom?

Answers to the trivia questions are on pages 196–198.

Blue was a prep phenom in Mansfield and very well could have accomplished that goal, but his mother needed money, so he signed with Oakland. Finley wooed him by phone. He signed for a $25,000 bonus plus some perks. He entered the minor league system, made a few brief big-league appearances to get a flavor for the thing, then provided a preview of coming attractions when he threw a no-hit game against division-champion Minnesota at the end of the 1970 season.

The A's entered the 1971 season as favorites to win the West. They were *stacked,* but the key was Blue. It did not look good after the opener when Vida was hammered by the Washington Senators in the Presidential Opener, 8–0. After that, Blue put on a stretch that may never be equaled. He won 10 straight, and it was one of the most impressive 10 straight in history. His first-half record of 17–3 at the All-Star break represents probably the best half-season pitching performance since the dead-ball era.

Some early-century twirlers like Walter Johnson, Christy Mathewson, and Cy Young put up those kinds of numbers. After World War II, one considers Guidry in 1978, Roger Clemens in 1986, and Orel Hershiser in the second half of 1988, but Vida's performance was as good as any of theirs.

When Vida started and was the winning pitcher of the 1971 All-Star Game, he had a legitimate shot at winning 30 games three years after Denny McLain did it in 1968. He became the biggest name in sports, overnight. His starts brought sellout crowds in Oakland and on the road, but the team failed to markedly increase attendance when Hunter or Odom pitched.

Blue threw total southpaw heat from a huge leg kick. His fastball was dubbed the "Blue blazer." But he was a semitragic figure, a flameout of sorts. History records that Hunter far surpasses Blue. Jackson was more important. Blue is not a Hall of Famer, not really close despite having very rare talent.

He was not a complete pitcher. The league caught on to his fastball and he trailed off in the second half of 1971, then blew a

En route to the Cy Young and MVP awards in 1971, Vida Blue's "Blue blazer" forged perhaps the greatest first-half season of pitching dominance ever.

IF ONLY . . . The players had not struck and Vida Blue had not held out, the 1972 A's may well have won closer to 110 regular-season games instead of the 93 they captured en route to the world title.

3–1 seventh-inning lead to Baltimore in the playoff opener, losing 5–3 en route to a disappointing sweep at the hands of the Orioles. He still finished 24–8 with a 1.82 earned-run average, 301 strikeouts, and eight shutouts. He earned league MVP and Cy Young honors.

Blue then made a huge error, holding out against the tightfisted Finley. In 1972 he did not report to spring training. He allowed himself to be made into a clown figure by accepting a job with a bathroom fixtures company, engendering a *Sports Illustrated* cover photo depicting him as a toilet-seat salesman. The fans turned on him, and worse, it quickly became obvious that the team's pitching (with new addition Kenny Holtzman) was so strong that they could go all the way without his services, which is basically what they did.

When Blue finally signed for a nominal raise, he had lost his edge. He pitched poorly all year, losing his starting role in a 6–10 season. His only contributions actually ended up being just the difference, however: four innings of lights-out relief to save a 2–1 win over Detroit, giving Oakland a nail-biter American League championship, then one good relief performance versus Cincinnati in the World Series. However, he was slammed, 8–1, in his Game 6 start.

Blue lost his innocence. In examining how baseball became a game of money, free agents, mercenaries, and fan-unfriendly miscreants, unfortunately two A's—Blue and Jackson, both of whom intimated racial prejudice in arguing their respective cases—play a large role in the transformation that festers to this day.

Vida was a good pitcher, but never as good as he could have been. He won 20 in 1973, he won a lot of games in Oakland and later in San Francisco, but his talent, which screamed "300-game winner and Hall of Famer," was not lived up to. Blue beat Jim Palmer 1–0 in a 1974 championship series win over Baltimore, but aside from that game and his 1972 relief appearances, he was unreliable in the post-season clutch. The comparison to "money" hurlers Hunter, Holtzman, and Fingers was impossible to ignore.

The irony of it all is that, despite a rough patch with the press and the fans, Vida is a truly nice man, but he battled inner demons, which included a bout with cocaine addiction. In many ways, he was a cautionary tale, but he was an extraordinary talent on a team of great talent.

The "Mustache Gang"

Longtime Bay Area sportswriter Ron Bergman wrote an entertaining paperback tome of the early 1970s A's called *Mustache Gang*. The A's of 1972 to 1974 (or of 1968 to 1976, depending on your standards) were one of the best teams ever and are certainly on an extremely short list of the most colorful.

The A's won three straight world championships (from 1972 to 1974) and five consecutive West Division titles (from 1971 to 1975). But the team was fairly well kept together from their arrival in Oakland in 1968 until 1976, the last season in which Finley "held the line" before losing the whole team to free agency. The A's were immediately successful, rising to the .500 level their first year. They contended for two years, won a division (but lost in the playoffs) before winning the three straight Series, then won another division (1975) before losing to Boston in the championship series. In 1976, with Reggie Jackson and Catfish Hunter gone, amidst turmoil surrounding free agency, "trades" that were disallowed by the commissioner, and the rise of the Kansas City Royals, the A's stayed in contention well into September but could not pull it off.

In 1977 nobody recognized the A's anymore. Amazingly, they played brilliant ball throughout the first month of that season, leading to speculation that they might be able to maintain their winning ways, but the jig was up. Three years of losing separate the "Mustache Gang" from "Billy Ball."

When it comes to on-field success, Oakland's historical ranking can be argued. How much better or worse they were than Ruth's Murderers' Row Yankees of the 1920s, the Gehrig-DiMaggio Yankees of the 1930s, the Stengel-Mantle Yankees of the 1950s, the

Mantle-Maris Yankees of the 1960s, the Jackson-Guidry Yankees of the 1970s, or the Jeter-Torre Yankees of the 1990s is debatable. Let us just say the A's could hold their own. Whether they were the best A's team ever assembled is also questionable, considering Connie Mack's juggernauts of 1910 through 1914 and 1929 through 1931. Were they better than the Big Red Machine of the 1970s? When they played Cincinnati they beat 'em! On paper is just on paper. Between the lines, they took on all comers and were victorious.

As for the issue of colorful characters, in this regard they may be the most unique of all teams, even more so than St. Louis's Gashouse Gang of the 1930s, Brooklyn's Boys of Summer in the 1950s, or the Yankees' Bronx Zoo in the 1970s.

The man who announced the A's "phantasmagorical" events over the radio was a homespun Oklahoman named Monte Moore. Nobody will ever confuse Monte with Vin Scully, Ernie Harwell, or Bill King. He was said to be Charlie O.'s gofer, a spy of sorts who told the boss what the players said about him behind his back. The players considered him to be a yes-man who carried out all of

From left, Mike Epstein, Dave Duncan, Joe Rudi, and "Cap'n Sal" Bando celebrate the first of three straight world titles in 1972.

TOP 10

A's Teams

1. 1929 Philadelphia
2. 1930 Philadelphia
3. 1974 Oakland
4. 1989 Oakland
5. 1910 Philadelphia
6. 1972 Oakland
7. 1911 Philadelphia
8. 1913 Philadelphia
9. 1973 Oakland
10. 1931 Philadelphia

Finley's orders no matter how distasteful and whose loyalties were directed entirely toward the owner, not the team or the players he described.

It was rumored that Monte said over the air what Charlie told him to say. Moore was a nice guy with a fun personality, but he was a bit of a yahoo, employing over-the-top use of exclamations and descriptions that may not have been dictionary-friendly. When Rollie Fingers came on to save the game it was "hold 'em Rollie Fingers time." A Reggie Jackson homer was a "tater." Vida's fastball was a "Blue blazer."

Monte—not Harry Caray—was just right for the A's, though. Their fan base in the '70s was more of a cult. They switched radio stations regularly, sometimes finding themselves with poor signal wattage. It was a low-rent show, absent any bells and whistles.

For a while, another Finley yes-man shared the A's broadcast booth. Jimmy Piersall was truly unstable mentally when he broke in with the Boston Red Sox of the early 1950s. Apparently driven half-mad by his domineering father, he lost it on the field, climbing halfway up the Fenway Park backstop during a game. The mental hospital apparently cured him enough for him to return and play a fine career in which he was considered a superior defensive center fielder—when he was not nose-snubbing or flipping off fans!

Fear Strikes Out, a movie detailing his early-career events, starred Anthony Perkins (*Psycho*) as Piersall and Karl Malden as his intense father. Piersall hated it. Who would want his life portrayed by Tony Perkins? Piersall was not afraid to air his feelings. When he was the Chicago White Sox announcer, he publicly declared that baseball players' wives were "just a bunch of horny broads."

When he was with the A's, however, Piersall did Charlie's bidding, no questions asked. His on-air comments sounded more like one of Caesar's heralds proclaiming the emperor's greatness while the prisoners from Gaul were paraded into the Colosseum.

But in 1972 the A's dispelled all the talk about their funny uniforms, white shoes, long hair, "homer" announcers, paltry attendance, unkempt stadium operations, lack of security, cheap travel arrangements, dumpin' donkey, angry clubhouse, and eccentric owner.

The season got off to a bad start when the players went on strike for the first seven games of the year. Manager Dick Williams's crew picked up from their 101-win campaign of the previous season determined to take it to the next level. Early in the season, Denny McLain, a 31-game winner four years earlier in Detroit, pitched in their rotation. It was quickly made obvious that his troubles (gambling, weight gain, sore arm, troubled marriage, tax evasion, and racketeering, just to name a few) had reduced his ability to pitch effectively.

The loss of Blue to a prolonged holdout never stopped them. Ken Holtzman came over from the Cubs in exchange for the popular Rick Monday. An All-American at the University of Illinois, Holtzman had starred under Leo Durocher in Chicago. His A's teammates immediately dubbed him "Jew," which was probably politically incorrect enough to create a civil lawsuit on another team, but with the freewheelin' A's it was just another nickname. Jewish athletes are a rarity, but the A's had two. First baseman Mike Epstein from L.A.'s Fairfax High and Cal-Berkeley

TRIVIA

When Vida Blue held out in 1972, Charlie O. Finley pulled a major psychological move. Which superstar pitcher of the 1960s was acquired in order to send the message to Blue that he could be replaced?

Answers to the trivia questions are on pages 196–198.

looked like a Mossad enforcer with his long hair, handlebar mustache, and hulking frame. He was nicknamed "Super Jew."

Holtzman was 19–11 with a 2.51 earned-run average. Catfish Hunter was 21–7 with a 2.04 ERA. John "Blue Moon" Odom, when not fighting with Vida Blue or anybody else who took exception to his prickly personality, was 15–6 with a 2.50 ERA. Rollie Fingers saved 21 games with a 2.51 ERA. Bob Locker (2.65 ERA) and Darold Knowles (1.36 ERA) rounded out the bullpen. Even Blue, 6–10 out of the pen and making spot starts in his worst year, had a 2.80 earned-run average.

Nobody could score on the A's! Between starters and relievers, the A's of this era may have had the best pitching *ever*. The 1954 Indians, the Koufax-Drysdale Dodgers, the 1969–1971 Orioles, the Braves of the 1990s, and the A's of the 2000s: great pitching, but few, if any, were better. Historians have to go back to the dead-ball era, when Christy Mathewson and Joe McGinnity toiled for New York, to find skewed statistics that are better.

They were a team of defensive gems. Left fielder Joe Rudi quietly flagged down everything while hitting .305, considered a big average in those pitcher-rich days. Reggie mostly played center field that year, and his 25 homers, 75 RBIs, and .265 average nearly earned him the MVP award (Chicago's Dick Allen got it).

At 93–62 they took on Billy Martin and Detroit in the playoffs. The first two games in Oakland went the A's way, although shortstop Campy Campaneris managed to get himself suspended for the rest of the series when he *threw his bat* at Tigers reliever Lerrin LaGrow after a brushback pitch. Campaneris was permitted to play in the World Series and then was suspended for the first 10 games of the '73 season.

Martin went out of his mind. His team lost that game, 5–0, but they were fired up when the series moved to raucous Tiger Stadium.

The hostile crowds were more like English or Latin American soccer hooligans: a combination of racial tensions, borderline criminality, and old-fashioned home-team pride.

Oakland looked to have escaped with a three-games-to-one triumph when the team took an extra-inning lead in Game 4, but Williams had substituted his second basemen so many times (on Finley's orders) that he had catcher Gene Tenace playing the position. Tenace dropped a throw on a sure force-out, giving Detroit life in a 4–3 upset.

Game 5 was one of the most harrowing in baseball history. Detroit fans pelted the field with garbage, some of it lethal. This is their style. In 1934 they nearly rioted in protest of Cardinals outfielder Ducky Medwick's hard, spikes-up slide an inning earlier.

In 1972 memories of Detroit's race riots in 1967 and Martin Luther King's 1968 assassination (which had postponed a number of baseball openers that April) were still fresh. Oakland outfielder George Hendrick was pelted with debris, as was Jackson. Had Campaneris been on the field after his bat-tossing incident, all hell might have broken loose.

Odom got in a fight with Blue before the game, which was all the inspiration he required in a tight five-inning, one-run performance. Then he handed the ball off to Blue as if they were blood brothers. Blue held Detroit scoreless for four innings, amid the madness of the increasingly hostile crowd. Williams knew he needed to manufacture a run, so he called for a "steal-and-go" play on a first-and-third situation. Jackson beat the return throw, evading catcher Bill Freehan. His torn hamstring kept him out of the World Series, but the team was at first just happy to be there.

"This is a game that requires no description," TV announcer Jim Simpson said. Amid intolerable tensions, Blue mowed down Detroit's veteran hitters—Freehan, Jim Northrup, Al Kaline, Willie Horton—until none was left standing except the celebrating A's. A sullen city skulked home to hibernate for the winter.

The Hairs versus the Squares

Cincinnati was waiting at Riverfront Stadium. They were the prohibitive favorites.

"The secret here is they underrate us," said Sal Bando. "They don't think we're ballplayers, they think we're bananas," referring to their funky uniforms. "The hairs versus the squares" provided a snapshot of society in 1972. Cincinnati was one of the most conservative cities in America. Oakland was the home of free love, antiwar protests, and the Black Panthers. The uniforms of the two teams provided a contrast that would make Salvador Dalí cringe.

The Reds wore traditional, plain white-and-red uniforms. A banner at Riverfront Stadium told their story: "Women's lib will destroy the family" (this was while abortion was a huge national issue, with the Supreme Court hearing the *Roe v. Wade* case they would decide a few months later). They featured the old-style high socks (naturally, only when they went out of style did they actually go into style with many players in the late 1990s). Cincinnati wore plain black shoes, the A's white spikes. The A's: long hair, beards, mustaches, sideburns, funk. The Reds: shorn, shaved, Norman Rockwell.

Reds manager Sparky Anderson was from the old school, having grown up in an L.A. house that was eventually torn down to make way for the building of Dedeaux Field, the gleaming baseball stadium at the University of Southern California. Two recent A's, Marcel and Rene Lachemann, had played at USC after playing at Anderson's alma mater, Dorsey High School. Rumor has it that Sparky, a one-time Trojan batboy, slept in a bedroom situated where home plate at Dedeaux Field now is.

Anderson's proximity to higher learning did not prevent him from destroying the English language, but he knew how to run a baseball team. His way. Dick Williams had grown up playing high school ball for one of Dorsey's rivals, Fremont. He, too, knew how to run a team—his way—but he also had to adhere to Charlie O.'s way, which was already causing tensions.

The Reds dominated the National League West before winning a cliff-hanger in five games against defending world champion Pittsburgh. When the A's and Reds met to open the Series on a Saturday afternoon in Cincinnati, they resembled winners of triathlons meeting the next day to run a marathon.

The Reds "looked over at the hairy young A's, in their outlandish green-and-gold costumes, with patronizing curiosity that was perhaps shared by a great majority of baseball fans everywhere," wrote the fabulous Roger Angell in *Five Seasons*. The Reds, wrote Angell, were "as clean and barefaced as Kiwanians" who could not hide "the evident conviction that their most dangerous opponents of the year had already been buried." Indeed, both survivors were "less aroused about the games to come than relieved about the ones past," wrote Angell.

The intensity of both leagues' playoffs probably played to Oakland's advantage. The huge Cincinnati crowds were not as crazy. The Reds felt the right to relax a bit. The A's were so happy just to be there, the pressure valve of emotion having been lifted, that they felt the right to take on the fall classic in a loosey-goosey manner. Two

DID YOU KNOW . . . That six people who participated in the 1972 World Series are now in the Hall of Fame? Catfish Hunter and Rollie Fingers of the A's and Johnny Bench, Joe Morgan, Tony Perez, and Manager Sparky Anderson of Cincinnati are all members of the Hall. However, before all is said and done, as many as nine could end up at Cooperstown. This includes Oakland manager Dick Williams, plus the Reds' Dave Concepcion and, of course, the controversial Pete Rose. Hall of Famer Reggie Jackson of the A's missed the Series with an injured hamstring suffered when he scored the winning run in the championship series clincher.

things helped their cause. First, Ken Holtzman, Catfish Hunter, and Rollie Fingers were "lights out." History tells us that Hunter and Fingers are two of the all-time greats. This was not yet an established fact in October 1972, but it would be. The underrated Holtzman, while not a fellow Hall of Famer, was a "money pitcher" of the first order.

Second, Cincinnati's bats went silent. The assortment of fastballs, sliders, and corner cutters the A's masters threw at them did not resemble the stuff of Bob Gibson, Tom Seaver, or even Vida Blue. They were lulled to sleep and lay there quietly while Oakland took the first two games.

Gene Tenace made history by homering in his first two at-bats of Game 1 to power Holtzman past the Reds, 3–2, with Blue reprising his closer's role in Detroit. Vida, still miffed over his salary hassles and the public humiliation that came with his ill-fated toilet-sales career, was about as mature as a 13-year-old. Whenever he opened his mouth, God only knew what would come out of it. He complained that he should be in the starting rotation, that he was being publicly insulted. Somehow he figured his 6–10 record was as worthy as Odom's 15 victories, Holtzman's brilliance, and Catfish's increasingly successful bid for immortality.

Speaking of Catfish's bid for immortality, he took, as Neil Armstrong might have said, one giant leap toward that end in the Sunday game when he silenced the Big Red Machine on six hits with last-out help from Rollie. It almost came to naught when Denis Menke's sure RBI, extra-base shot was nabbed in "snow cone" fashion by Rudi at the top of the high Riverfront left-field wall.

Cincinnati's Tony Perez just shook his head, refusing to acknowledge Hunter's greatness. The Reds were in shock after the 2–1 loss and two-game home sweep with three coming up on the West Coast. A proud crew, they also included left fielder Pete Rose, who it could be said liked to win. Catcher Johnny Bench, winner of his second MVP award in three years that season, was at the top of his game. He totally nullified the considerable speed of the A's. Shortstop Dave

TRIVIA

Who would not let Hank Aaron use his practice field because he would lose too many baseballs?

Answers to the trivia questions are on pages 196–198.

Hall of Famer Rollie Fingers (being mobbed) first made his mark closing out the Reds in Game 7 of the 1972 fall classic.

Concepcion was a glove genius. Second baseman Joe Morgan was one of the finest ever to play the position, eventually winning back-to-back Most Valuable Player awards and induction into Cooperstown.

The Reds' weak link was starting pitching. Their bullpen was strong. Anderson went to it early and often, but in the '72 Series, form was oddly reversed. Cincinnati's offensive juggernaut was stymied, but their pitchers, for the most part, carried them. While the comparison between baseball and other sports is not the easiest to make, Oakland's successful strategy in that Series seemed to be like a football team that keeps a powerful opposing offense off the field by playing ball control or a basketball team that is able to slow a fast-breaking foe off its game.

For Game 3 of the Series, the teams returned to Oakland. A funnel cloud left the entire Bay Area—from Santa Rosa to Livermore to San Jose—quite dry, all except for the Coliseum, where the baseball gods

By the NUMBERS **G: 7 R: 16 Avg.: .209**—Oakland's offensive output in winning the 1972 World Series on the strength of its pitching.

deemed it necessary to dump filthy loads of wet stuff. The game was rained out.

Finley's dream of night World Series games came to fruition in the form of one game between Baltimore and Pittsburgh the previous year, but in his own ballpark in 1972, all three games were played at night. The All-Star Game had gone under the lights for good beginning in 1970. The idea seemed to lack some merit in the California twilight when Jack Billingham of the Reds and John Odom of the A's looked more like Jim Palmer dueling Nolan Ryan. Nobody could see a thing in Cincinnati's 1–0 win. The highlight came late in the game with Bench at the plate, runners at second and third, and a 3–2 count on him. Williams consulted with Fingers, providing elaborate gyrations indicating that the only logical move was to walk the slugger. Bench stood like Casey at the bat, accepting his role as a batsman so feared that pitching to him was out of the question. Tenace stood, arm outstretched for the intentional pass. Then he crept back into his crouch while Fingers delivered what can only be described as "blue hammer," a wicked slider on the outside black. Mighty Johnny had struck out.

Tenace hit a homer the next night, and what seemed like an army of pinch-hitters came through with "seeing eye" singles in the ninth to lift Oakland to a 3–2 win.

With a chance to close it, Tenace hit his *fourth* homer of the Series the next day, putting himself in the same company as guys named Ruth and very few others. Hunter was off, but the A's pulled ahead, 4–2, only to watch Cincinnati chip away at their vaunted bullpen, namely the great Fingers. Now trailing 5–4, Oakland put pinch runner Odom on third with one out in the bottom of the ninth. A lazy pop drifted along the spacious right side, which has more open territory than any stadium. It might have been in the seats at Fenway Park or Yankee Stadium, but in Oakland Joe Morgan caught it over his shoulder like Paul Warfield, stumbled, then fired a strike to Bench. Odom, tagging, was out by a mile, but the A's had to take the chance. It took perfection from Morgan, and of course Bench picked it up and guarded home, looking to Blue Moon as impenetrable as the Secret Service guarding home plate. You are *out of here!*

Next game, they gave the ball to Blue, who told everyone with a pen or a microphone that he alone could stop the Reds in Game 6 at Cincinnati. He was as effective as the French Army circa 1940: 8–1, Reds. The worst possible sinking feeling hung over Oakland. The fact that they overcame that feeling to win the decider, 3–2, is the greatest testament to their fortitude, focus, and heart.

The win was a combination of Odom, Catfish, Holtzman, and a "lights out" Fingers (two scoreless innings for the save). The day before, Cincinnati ran on the A's like Jesse Owens. They finally swung their bats and looked unbeatable. Stemming that momentum required something few teams possess. Heart. Guts. Character.

The A's had won the World Series without Jackson. Blue was available but was not the Vida of other years. It was a perfect example of the old axiom that good pitching stops good hitting, or one of Mr. Mack's own truisms: "Baseball is 90 percent pitching."

It sure was in October 1972.

Reggie Takes Charge

The year 1973 was a strange one. It began with Richard Nixon bathed in the glory of a diplomatic opening to China, the successful triangulation of peace accords with the North Vietnamese, and a nuclear-reduction deal with the Soviets driven by their fear of our new relationship with China. On top of this, Nixon's second term began with the support of 49 states and 62 percent of the electorate.

By the time spring training was in full swing in March, the Watergate hearings had begun. By year's end there was "a cancer on the presidency," Nixon's deals with Russia were in jeopardy, his peace accords (and his presidency) headed to the ash heap of history when Ted Kennedy and the Democrats refused to live up to them.

The A's were quite familiar with Nixon, a big baseball fan from the L.A. area who had invited Vida Blue and company to the White House in 1971 during a series with the Senators. Nixon had instituted very un-Republican price controls. When Sal Bando asked if that meant Charlie O. Finley was prohibited from giving them raises, Nixon replied, to Blue, "Well, that means he can't give you more gas for your car," which Finley had just bought him as a midseason bonus. "I've read you're the most underpaid player in baseball. I wouldn't like to be the lawyer negotiating your contract."

Oakland began the year as the prohibitive favorite. Catfish Hunter started the opener against Minnesota, and the Coliseum looked like a launching pad...of Twins home runs. Minnesota kept it up all series, leaving with a 3–0 sweep. The A's dynasty of the early 1970s saw them dominate the American League East and West. All except Minnesota. It was a strange carryover from 1969 and 1970.

In those years, the veteran Twins won the West with 97 and 98 wins, respectively. The A's won 88 and 89, respectively. Much of the difference came in their dismal 5–13 record against Minnesota both years. The eight-game differential made up eight of the nine games separating the teams in both seasons. If the 88–74 A's of 1969 could have finished 10–8 versus Minnesota (five more wins out of 18 played), they would have been 93–69, the Twins 92–70. The same result in 1970 would have won them the West at 94–69 versus the Twins' 93–70.

The Twins had been exceptionally frustrating. In 1969–1970 Oakland would get a winning streak going, coming within three games of Minnesota heading into a series against the Twins. After the Minnesota sweep, the six-game difference would look insurmountable

Bert Campaneris (left) and Reggie Jackson helped make up the disparate elements of the A's dynasty of the 1970s. Photo courtesy of AP/Wide World Photos.

and prove in the end to be just that. Minnesota beat the A's at the Coliseum and at Metropolitan Stadium. They probably would have beaten them on a playground.

The Twins, a talented team with Harmon Killebrew, Tony Oliva, Rod Carew, and Jim Perry in the 1960s, got very old very fast in 1971, but they continued to give the superior young A's trouble in their championship years, as if reserving all their energy for the team they once schooled.

With the initial Minnesota debacle over, however, Oakland's staff was airtight—except when they played the Twins. But the A's recovered, thanks in large part to the reemergence of Vida Blue (20–9, 3.28 ERA). He was a different pitcher and person from the man-child of 1971—tempered by bitter disputes with Charlie, matured by failure. He still threw heat but allowed his defense to pick up the slack. He was not the strikeout artist of old, but his pitch counts were lower.

The amazing A's staff had two other 20-game winners: Hunter (21–5, 3.34 ERA) and Ken Holtzman (21–13, 2.97). Holtzman threw 90 percent fastballs. He fooled nobody, beating them anyway. One of the most fabulous modern staffs in baseball history was rounded out by superior relievers, anchored by Rollie Fingers (22 saves, 1.92 ERA). No reliever had ever won the Cy Young Award, but when Fingers starred in Oakland, Kansas City manager Whitey Herzog opined that Fingers was the MVP of the whole league. He revolutionized the role of relief pitchers in baseball!

The A's had won it all with little offense in 1972, but in 1973 their bats came alive, led by Jax with 32 home runs, 117 runs batted in, and a .293 batting average. It was good enough to earn him the Most Valuable Player award, but he still had to fight for Finley's dollars. The owner noted that Jackson's power numbers went down in 1972 (25

DID YOU KNOW . . . That the 1973 World Series was the "last hurrah" of Willie Mays? His mishandling easy bouncing singles, falling down chasing fly balls, and begging an umpire for a call reversal on his knees are the unfortunate final images of his great career.

homers) from his 1971 numbers (32) and that he was down in 1973 from his 1969 numbers (47 homers, 118 RBIs). It was always something.

"You'd sit down with Charlie," he once said, "and he'd say, 'Why, this man hit 15 fewer home runs than he

TRIVIA

How many Hall of Famers were involved in the 1973 World Series?

Answers to the trivia questions are on pages 196–198.

had in this previous season' or 'Why should I pay a man more to hit seven fewer homers' or 'He drove in 118 runs in 1969 and only 117 in 1973, why that's not improvement!' I'd walk out of those meetings just saying, 'Why, I must be horses——t!'"

In 1973, with or without Finley's acknowledgment, Jackson took a big step toward Cooperstown, New York. Ray Fosse came over from Cleveland to take over behind the plate. Freed from catching, Gene Tenace hit 24 homers, as if his four "taters" in the '72 Series had taught him he was capable of the act. Dick Green emerged from a veritable sea of revolving second basemen to establish himself as one of the best glove men in the game. Bando had, all things considered, his best season (29 home runs, 98 RBIs, and a .287 average). Campaneris played adequate defense and stole key bases. New center fielder Billy North also was a speedster.

In analyzing the success of the A's, it is apparent their speed was a key ingredient. The American League was considered the inferior circuit before the A's dynasty. The Yankee way—long balls and arrogance—had not transferred to the rest of the AL. Baltimore lost two of three World Series to teams considered below their talent level. The difference: "National League baseball"—a euphemism for fast, aggressive black and Latino ballplayers from Jackie Robinson of Brooklyn to Willie Mays of the Giants to Roberto Clemente of Pittsburgh to Lou Brock of St. Louis—had made the senior circuit the better league. But Finley did not play it the Yankee way, and his way paid dividends.

Kansas City asserted its presence with 88 victories, but Oakland won the division without being pushed, notching 94 wins. Baltimore manager Earl Weaver, he of the old "wait-around-until-someone-hits-a-three-run-homer" school that had landed him on the losing end against the Mets (1969) and the Pirates (1971), also adapted in

IF ONLY . . . Mike Andrews had not made two errors in the same inning to hand New York Game 2 of the 1973 World Series, his once-promising career might not have come to an abrupt end. A Southern Californian, Andrews came up as a young star on Dick Williams's 1967 Boston champions. His brother, Rob, played for the Astros and Giants.

1973. Rich Coggins and Al Bumbry played National League baseball, their speed lifting the Orioles past the inertia of aging sluggers Boog Powell and Brooks Robinson. Jim Palmer (22–9, 2.40 ERA) was at the top of his form in winning the Cy Young Award, and at 97–65 Baltimore figured to give the A's all they were worth.

When Palmer outclassed Blue, 6–0, in the opener, it looked that way, but the A's had the ability to pull it together, as they had done the year before after losing two straight to Detroit and Cincinnati before rebounding. Hunter beat Dave McNally, 6–3. Holtzman out-dueled Mike Cuellar, 2–1. Then Blue led Palmer, 4–0, through six, but Blue blew his lead and Fingers gave up a home run to Bobby Grich, so instead of a 3–1 ALCS win it was 2–2. Hunter shut down the O's, 3–0, in the decider. Baltimore had as much chance with Catfish as a one-legged man in a butt-kickin' contest, and the championship belonged to the A's.

The World Series looked to be a rematch with Cincinnati, but when the 82–79 Mets beat the Reds in the NLCS, Oakland found itself the heavy favorite. Form held with Oakland's Game 1 victory, but when the sloppy A's let New York capture the second contest, a sense of unreality settled over the Coliseum, which was bathed in that wonderful Indian summer heat that is a Bay Area October.

The Mets had little outside of superior pitching: Jon Matlack and Jerry Koosman, ace lefties, and irrepressible reliever Tug McGraw. Then there was Tom Seaver, baseball's best hurler of the era, a guy Reggie Jackson said was "so good blind people come to the park to hear him pitch."

Outside of Sandy Koufax in the mid-1960s, Bob Gibson in 1968, Orel Hershiser in 1988, and maybe Lefty Grove or Walter Johnson in a bygone era, nobody has ever dominated like Seaver. His teams, figuring he would pitch a 14-inning shutout if that's what it took, generally scored a run for him every month or so. His win-loss records do not reflect his dominance, which is why Reggie and the A's performances against him were so remarkable.

In sloppy fashion, the Mets and A's split the first two games of the World Series 1–1 in Oakland. Charlie O. managed to make an ass out of himself by "firing" second baseman Mike Andrews for making two errors. It was the kind of distraction that other teams use as an excuse to lose. Not so these A's.

Under chilly night skies at Shea Stadium, Seaver (finally rested after besting the Reds in the playoffs) was staked to a 2–0 lead, which seemed more like 12–0 while he struck out 12. But the A's chipped away, using Campy's speed, to tie it at 2–2. With Seaver gone, Oakland managed to win it 3–2 in 11, but Matlack and Koosman shut the door in Games 2 and 3 (one run in 18 innings).

For Game 6, they were back to the hot sunshine of Oakland and a personal duel between 1965 collegians: USC's Seaver versus Arizona State's Jackson, who with fellow Sun Devil Bando added the '73 World Series to the '65 College World Series and '72 World Series already under their belts. Seaver mowed the A's down with precision—all except Jackson, whose two RBI doubles and a single proved just enough of a chink in the tired Seaver's armor. Final: 3–1, Oakland.

The next day, the momentum had swung beyond New York's power to stem it. They were like the Wehrmacht once Patton's tanks rescued Bastogne—just playing out the string. Reggie personally handled business: a two-run smash spurring a four-run third, Holtzman and Fingers stopping the Mets cold, Darold Knowles closing it out for a 5–2 world championship win.

The irritations of the team, the Andrews "firing," and the players' mutual dislike of old man Finley soured the whole thing. The last symbolic act was Williams quitting because he could not take another middle-of-the-night phone call from a guy listening to the radio in an Indiana farmhouse.

A Rare Thing

It has often been said that there are very few Jewish athletes, although there are exceptions, and sometimes big ones. First, there were a fair number of Jewish boxers in early 20th-century America. It was a way out of poverty. Sports became a manner of assimilation into American society, especially in Brooklyn, where the Dodgers were beloved in the borough's large Jewish community.

Hank Greenberg was a great baseball star of the 1930s. Art Shamsky was a good platoon outfielder and pinch-hitter for the Mets. Shawn Green was a power hitter.

The all-time greatest Jewish athlete is Sandy Koufax. Brooklyn born, he rose to stardom in L.A., where there is a large Jewish population. A few years after "Dandy Sandy," Ken Holtzman came along.

Traded by the Cubs to the A's for Rick Monday, Holtzman found himself in a clubhouse full of blacks, Dominicans, Venezuelans, Cubans, Italians, urbanites, Southern good ol' boys, hell raisers, and evangelical Christians. He fit right in. Finley, he of California by way of Alabama by way of Chicago by way of Indiana, assembled a team the UN would be proud of.

Naturally, Holtzman was assigned a nickname. Everybody else had one. The pitching staff had a "Catfish" and a "Blue Moon" (although "True" Blue resisted that moniker). Naturally, Kenny's handle was "Jew."

"I don't think anyone means much by it," he stated. "I'm not ashamed of being Jewish. I guess a Jewish player stands out because there aren't many. Sandy Koufax was Jewish. He was also left-handed. He may have been a little better than I am," he laughed.

The whole "Jews don't make good athletes" concept was thrown on its head by Koufax and Holtzman, who joined forces with still another Jewish player already on the A's. First baseman Mike Epstein was a big, burly ex–football player at California. *His* nickname: "Super Jew." Only on the Swingin' A's.

It is sad to say, but anti-Semitism did play a part in Holtzman's career, just not in Oakland. His manager in Chicago was Leo

Southpaw Kenny Holtzman was a clutch twirler for the A's.

Durocher. It would not be fair to call Leo a bigot. He was an urbane fellow from the Frank Sinatra school, but he had a big mouth and, like Sinatra, when he started talking anything could come out.

Holtzman gave him the benefit of the doubt, saying that by the time he got to the major leagues, baseball was "not getting a lot of players from small towns in the South anymore." Players were more intelligent by the late 1960s; many had college degrees.

"Leo believed we should eat, drink, and sleep baseball," said Holtzman. "He didn't understand that there was life beyond baseball."

Ken actually did not want to go into baseball, preferring to become a successful businessman, but he figured the money would help him build a base for the future.

Holtzman twice won 17 games for the Cubs, and stardom was predicted for him, but the team always fell short. Durocher and owner Phil Wrigley blamed players like Holtzman for not being dedicated enough. Holtzman asked to be traded.

After departing the A's, he became a Yankee, where he ran into real anti-Semitism courtesy of the unfortunate Billy Martin. When Martin called him "the Jew" it had none of the good-natured vibes of his A's teammates. He sounded more like Joe Pesci when he turns on Robert DeNiro in *Casino*. Billy's problems with people of Hebrew descent caught up to him under the Jewish ownership of the A's in the early 1980s.

In Oakland Holtzman was teased about his intellectuality and referred to as "the Thinker," but he told writer Bill Libby, "The guys can kid me all they want, I don't take it seriously. I live my own life."

TRIVIA

Tragic baseball figure Tony Conigliaro, whose career came to an end as a result of vision problems caused by a beanball incident, had Bay Area connections. What were they?

Answers to the trivia questions are on pages 196–198.

Holtzman was 19–11 with a 2.51 ERA (1972), 21–13 with a 2.97 ERA (1973), and 19–17 with a 3.07 ERA (1974). That record would be worth about $20 million in today's marketplace.

He was an unusual pitcher who threw about 90 percent fastballs. He certainly threw hard, but not hard enough to get away with

DID YOU KNOW . . . That the A's dynasty of the 1970s consisted of a larger-than-normal contingent of former major college players, among them Reggie Jackson (Arizona State), Sal Bando (Arizona State), Rick Monday (Arizona State), Ken Holtzman (Illinois), Mike Epstein (California), Ray Fosse (Southern Illinois–Carbondale), Rene Lachemann (USC), and Marcel Lachemann (USC)? The trend toward collegians was new at the time. Players like Tom Seaver (USC), Carl Yastrzemski (Notre Dame), and Jim Lonborg (Stanford) had recently enjoyed success. Today, Billy Beane is known to prefer collegians.

an all-fastball diet. But he spotted it up and down, using his defense successfully.

Holtzman and Hunter are a one-two postseason clutch-pitching duo of unparalleled dimensions. In the 1972, 1973, and 1974 winning playoff series, Ken was 2–1 but had several spectacular performances without a decision in games won by the A's. In 24 innings he gave up 12 hits, struck out 12, walked five, and had a 1.13 ERA.

In three World Series he was 4–1 with a 2.55 ERA. Holtzman might have been a Hall of Fame–quality pitcher, but in the wake of Oakland's breakup he ended up in bad situations, most notably with Martin in New York. He was not one to put up with that for long, leaving the game to pursue other opportunities when he still had a few good years left.

The Price of Respect

October 1974: so, here are the Oakland A's. They have won two consecutive World Series, defeating the formidable Big Red Machine and the invincible Tom Seaver. They have beaten Earl Weaver's Orioles of Palmer, Cuellar, and McNally. They have two players (Jackson and Hunter) who are very close to Hall of Fame status already and a third (Fingers) who has all the earmarks of Cooperstown himself. It would seem that, like other great juggernauts of American sports—the recent repeat national champion football teams at USC, the old Celtics, the Yankees—this would engender for them mythical status, media mega-attention, and respect bordering on outright fear from all opponents.

All, apparently, except the Los Angeles Dodgers. In 1972 Sparky Anderson's Reds were amused by Oakland's uniforms and so worn out by Pittsburgh that they took a lax attitude into the Series, but they respected Oakland. The Dodgers were one arrogant group, like they *were* baseball: their Taj Mahal stadium, their hallowed traditions, their adoring fans pouring in by the millions. Then there was their venerable Vin Scully, like a historian describing the British Empire's triumphs in real time.

The Dodgers had broken Jackie Robinson into the big leagues, putting themselves squarely on the right side of history. They had been a great team, just shy of dynasty status, in the 1950s. Then they moved to L.A. Owner Walter O'Malley pulled the wool over Giants owner Horace Stoneham's eyes. O'Malley got the warm lands of SoCal, a population with room to grow. Stoneham got the fog and bays, stopping growth at the water's edge.

O'Malley played at the L.A. Coliseum, a football stadium holding 90,000 profit-exploding customers, instead of the minor league version of Wrigley Field, holding 22,000; Stoneham got Seals Stadium and their 20,000 seats. Then O'Malley built baseball's greatest gem, Dodger Stadium, on a hilltop overlooking downtown L.A. Stoneham, for his part, went to Candlestick Point at 10:00 in the morning, proclaiming the place suitable because there was room for a parking lot he planned to build on a crooked landfill deal with Mayor George Christopher, which of course meant when the "Big One" hit, the place would be as vulnerable as Blanche duBois in *A Streetcar Named Desire*. By 3:00 PM he was cocktailing while the point was under siege from a windstorm that would have hemmed in the First Infantry Division.

The Giants were good. The Dodgers were always better. When the Giants played bridesmaid, the Koufax-Drysdale Dodgers were newlyweds in Hollywood, sweeping the New York Yankees, going to three World Series in four years. They were legends of the green plains of Dodger Stadium, a baseball version of Notre Dame in the West, as popular as Trojan football in L.A.

They had a few down years, but in 1974 Los Angeles knocked the Big Red Machine out of first place in the manner of Wellington over Napoleon. With great pitching, power, speed, and attitude, Los Angeles dominated the league, playing unbeatable ball in April and May, then surviving a few rough patches. When Cincinnati came to reclaim the prize, they found Dodger Stadium to be their Waterloo. One hundred and two wins. Andy Messersmith, Don Sutton, and a kinesiology professor, Mike Marshall, out of the bullpen. Marshall was as elitist as the House of Windsor, claiming to have mastered the physical art of pitching but in a way no ordinary Joe could understand.

By the NUMBERS **2**—The number of major league franchises to win three or more consecutive world championships. They include the New York Yankees, who did it three times (from 1936 to 1939, 1949 to 1953, and 1998 to 2000), and the Oakland Athletics (from 1972 to 1974).

The Infield (the caps are there for a reason): Steve Garvey, Davey Lopes, Ron Cey, and Bill Russell. Jimmy Wynn's last hurrah: 32 home runs and 108 RBIs in center, with Bill Buckner (.314), a guy who could wake up at midnight on New Year's Eve and hit a line drive in left.

Oakland? They coasted in at 90–72 in a division nobody else could win. The Hollywood Dodgers definitely were not impressed. Oakland beat Baltimore again, but it was nothing compared to the way Los Angeles schooled Pittsburgh.

The two-time repeat champs all seemingly had off years. Vida Blue won 17 but lost 15. Ken Holtzman was a game shy of 20 wins but

What this photo does not show is second baseman Dick Green's incredible grab of a sure hit, which he flipped to Bert Campaneris, who is shown here turning it into a clutch double play to end Game 4 of the 1974 World Series against Los Angeles. Photo courtesy of AP/Wide World Photos.

only two games better than .500. Jackson started like a house afire but slumped to 29 homers, 93 RBIs, and a .289 batting average. Guys like Joe Rudi just did not have the swagger that impressed those Dodgers. It was the infantry against the aviators, *The Naked and the Dead* versus *Top Gun.*

Lost in the shuffle was Tenace with his 26 homers, Campy at .290, North and his base stealing, the unknown Dick Green making the right side of the infield an impenetrable fortress. Bando was supposedly on the way down, except that when nobody was looking he drove in 103 runs, 97 (or so) coming in key late-inning situations. Rollie Fingers was more untouchable than ever.

Then there was Catfish, the Cy Young winner with 25 wins and a 2.49 earned-run average. The Dodgers scoffed. *They* had Messersmith with his high cheese and Sutton with an "Uncle Charley" that started at the mezzanines and finished in those below-sea-level Chavez Ravine dugout seats.

Dodgers manager Walter Alston, a class act in the mold of John Wooden, tried to keep his charges on the straight and narrow, but their souls had been lost to third-base coach Tommy Lasorda, who had managed most of them at Ogden and Spokane. Tommy was a braggart who within a minute of meeting you told you he had Frank Sinatra's home phone number and a waiting table at some Hollywood eatery with food inedible by Original Joe's standards. In the manner of his constant "it's all about me" style, Tommy allowed himself to be hooked up to a microphone when the Series moved to Oakland. He babbled endlessly with third-base umpire Ron Luciano, attempting to explain why the Dodger way and National League baseball were superior products. Meanwhile, the A's pounded his boys into submission, therefore proving his thesis wrong just as he was making it.

After splitting two in Tinseltown, the teams came to Oakland. This location shoot put off Hollywood's box-office superstars, who lost three straight to a superior champion for the ages. Two plays—and two players—exemplified their hubris. The first was Marshall, the second Buckner.

Marshall had a doctorate from Michigan State University. He claimed that his studies of kinesiology had taught him that pitchers did not need to rest; rather, they needed to keep pitching. Whether Marshall's theses were valid or not, baseball people have not picked up on them in the years since, but in his prime Marshall was highly effective when used in this manner.

In 1974, however, he was outstanding. Alston used him in 106 games, pitching him not just to close games, but in mop-up and middle relief, too. He was 15–12, striking out 143 in 208 innings (a number most regular starters do not achieve) with a 2.42 ERA and 21 saves, earning him the Cy Young Award.

In Game 2 Marshall picked the A's Herb Washington off first base, an embarrassment for Finley, who had hired the non-baseball-playing sprinter strictly as a pinch runner. It saved the 3–2 victory, L.A.'s last hurrah. The Series shifted to the Bay Area. In recent years the Dodgers' superiority over the Giants had been made painfully obvious. Perhaps this regional snobbery made the Dodgers feel they would conquer Oakland as they had their cross-bay National League rivals. Fat chance.

TRIVIA

The 1974 World Series was the first all-California Series. How many World Series have been played between teams in the same state?

Answers to the trivia questions are on pages 196–198.

The A's won Games 3 and 4 and were trying to close it out in Game 5. With the score tied, 2–2, the Oakland fans got rowdy, directing much of their enthusiasm at Dodgers left fielder Bill Buckner. A timeout was called to let the ground crew pick up toilet paper and other unpleasantries. The Dodgers observed this spectacle in silent contemplation of the fact that their upscale fans did not engage in such tomfoolery.

Marshall was in, relieving the great Don Sutton. He stood off to the side, hands on his hips, as if to announce, "I'm so good I don't need a warm-up." He eschewed any tosses, choosing to square off with the clutch Joe Rudi. Rudi observed Marshall, concluded that without any warm-ups the first pitch would be a fastball, and, guessing just right, met it squarely for a solo home run.

His team trailing by a run, Buckner led off the eighth with a single. Billy North olé'd the ball, which went under his glove. Buckner, still an athlete (not the hobble-kneed defensive liability of

DID YOU KNOW . . . That weather patterns for the 1974 Oakland–Los Angeles World Series reversed form? L.A. was clear and bright. Oakland was hot and smoggy.

his 1986 Red Sox Series fiasco), went not just for second but tried to stretch it to third, breaking the ancient maxim, "Never make the first or third out at third base."

Jackson backed up North and fired to Green, who fired to Bando, who tagged out Buckner. It was the end for Los Angeles and a sad footnote to Buck's career. A Vallejo native, he retired just shy of 3,000 hits and was one of the game's very best hitters, but history shades him in Series failure.

Oakland became the only non-Yankees team in history to win three straight World Series.

Son of a Preacher Man

In many ways, the story of Alvin Dark is the story of America: a nation's reconciliation, redemption, and new understanding, followed by sociopolitical restructuring. This describes how the American South struggled to find, as Abe Lincoln called them, "the better angels of our nature." In many ways, through sports the South came to grips with new racial realities, then saw the Republican party husband the region "back into the Union" until they became not a marginalized New Deal voting bloc, but "rose again" to emerge as an economic and political powerhouse.

Al Dark was that walking conundrum of Dixie: the hardcore Baptist Christian burdened by racial prejudice. Through baseball, he was able to get out of the South and become a man of the world. It first led him to New York, where he starred for the 1954 world champion Giants. A great picture shows Dark and the black superstar Willie Mays, smiling in each other's company during the team's Broadway ticker tape parade.

Dark managed the greatest team in San Francisco Giants history. In 1962 the team came within one Willie McCovey line drive of winning the World Series, which has eluded the team in all their years on the West Coast (a fact that is even more exasperating when the team sees the four world title banners flying over the Coliseum). The Giants of the early 1960s were one of the first truly integrated teams. Mays, McCovey, Felipe Alou, Juan Marichal, and Orlando Cepeda were black and Latino stars of the first order.

Dark engendered controversy in 1963, when his team failed to repeat while the Dodgers raced to the world championship his Giants had just missed. Amid the disappointment, he stated in

TOP 10

Baseball Dynasties

1. 1921–1932 New York Yankees
2. 1947–1958 New York Yankees
3. 1936–1943 New York Yankees
4. 1996–2000 New York Yankees
5. 1972–1974 Oakland A's
6. 1910–1914 Philadelphia A's
7. 1912–1918 Boston Red Sox
8. 1960–1964 New York Yankees
9. 1929–1931 Philadelphia A's
10. 1904–1913 New York Giants

frustration that the blacks and Latinos were "a different kind" of player, to be handled with kid gloves, maybe not as likely to work hard or come through when the sledding got rough. When San Francisco gave way to Los Angeles and St. Louis, the more successful National League teams of the 1960s, Dark found himself on the outs. In cosmopolitan San Francisco, his way of doing things was seen as part of the past.

Charlie O. Finley was always part of the past, the present, and the future. Indeed, he had been born in Alabama before moving to the Midwest and then, of course, associating himself with the West Coast. He was an innovator who embraced New Age concepts like flashy colors, long hair, and the sexualization of culture. Although nobody ever could say he was a man of prejudice, he was a man of his surroundings and his past.

In 1966 Finley gave Dark another chance when he hired him to manage the Kansas City A's. Under Dark, the team improved. By 1967 much of the team's future foundation was in the system, either breaking into the majors or enjoying success in the minors. But Dark ran into trouble with Finley in the aftermath of the plane incident, when pitcher Lew Krausse had a bit too much to drink and took liberties with a stewardess. Finley accused Dark of colluding with the players in the drafting of their open letter to Finley.

Between 1:30 AM and 5:30 AM on a late August night in 1967, Dark and his coaching staff were fired, rehired, and fired again by Finley. Finley at first fired Dark because the players had supported him. Dark then "saved" his job by providing an optimistic, and ultimately prophetic, prediction of future championships with the young players under contract.

Dark, who had informed his coaches they had lost their jobs, called to say he had saved them after all. Then Finley called pitcher Jack Aker, a major instigator of the letter campaign. As fate would have it, Aker was not in his room, having broken curfew, a big no-no

Fired in San Francisco and considered by some to be a racist, the Southern, Christian Alvin Dark (talking to Reggie Jackson) was thought to be the wrong man in Oakland. That characterization changed when he took the helm of the 1974 world championship club.

for Finley. Finley apparently put Monte Moore on the hunt, looking for Aker in nearby watering holes or with a local baseball Annie.

Aker was finally produced, and like a prisoner hauled before the king, was taken to Finley's room. Moore provided the particulars of Aker's escapades, detailing them as if he were a private dick assigned to the case. Aker was in no moral position to argue his side, if indeed at 5:30 in

TRIVIA

In Game 1 of the 1974 World Series, Dodgers right fielder Joe Ferguson made one of the most spectacular throws in Series history to throw an A's runner out at home. What made the play unusual?

Answers to the trivia questions are on pages 196–198.

the morning he had the wherewithal to make any cogent points.

Then Aker, trying to save himself, said that Dark had been in on the letter, contradicting Dark's assertions that he had nothing to do with it. Apparently, Dark did possess knowledge of it before it was released, even though he did not help draft it and did not urge its release. Dark was fired, and Aker stayed with the team for the move to Oakland before being taken by the Seattle Pilots in the expansion draft following the 1968 season.

Dark managed in Cleveland with no success before getting rehired by Finley in 1974. Dick Williams, winner of consecutive world championships with the A's, had had enough of Finley's all-night phone interruptions and was hired by the Yankees. His dream job did not materialize; a contract could not be agreed upon between Williams and George Steinbrenner.

The world had changed drastically between 1967 and 1974. Al Dark looked like a dinosaur by this time. His Christian upbringing and Southern demeanor seemed more out of place than ever. In the Bay Area, the only "cool" Southerners were wild-eyed party animals like Ken Stabler and rockers like Lynyrd Skynyrd, who packed the Coliseum's "day on the green" concerts.

But it was precisely Dark's Christianity that allowed him to own up to his own flaws as a man. He pointed to biblical teachings, freely quoting New Testament verse in describing the transformation he had gone through in response to questions about his handling of minority players.

That with his solo blast in Game 4 of the 1974 World Series, Ken Holtzman became the only player to hit a World Series home run after having no base hits all season? He was also the 14th pitcher to homer in a Series game.

The A's were a free-wheelin' bunch, more like the Hell's Angels who were headquartered in Oakland than the "better angels of our nature." They were not a bad group. They pretty much stayed out of trouble, avoided police blotters and the like. Perhaps if they had played in New York their off-field habits would have been more exposed, but like the party-hearty Raiders, they benefited from the low-key Bay Area press corps. But they were no tent revival. Dark was. Sal Bando said Dark "couldn't manage a meat market."

How much Al Dark contributed to Oakland's 1974 world championship is debatable. Their regular-season record of 90–72 was in decline from those of the previous three seasons, but their postseason run was the best of any of those teams (Baltimore and the Dodgers falling like Poland during the Blitzkrieg). Dark benefited from a healthy roster of All-Stars and future Hall of Famers in their prime, which never hurts. This included one of the most airtight pitching staffs, top to bottom, in the history of the game. But like Pat Riley in Los Angeles and Phil Jackson in Chicago, credit must be given to coaches who did not screw it all up, because many others with talent-laden clubs have done just that.

Catfish

When people think of the great A's teams of the Finley era, Reggie Jackson often symbolizes their success, and for good reason. But Oakland won it with pitching: overwhelming, stifling, first-class pitching. They won the 1972 Series without Reggie but would not have won it without Catfish Hunter and his fellow mound stalwarts. In 1975 Oakland again won the West Division in impressive fashion but lost three straight to Boston in the playoffs. They had Reggie, but not Catfish.

There are a few men who are known as great "money pitchers." Lefty Gomez, Whitey Ford, Sandy Koufax, and Bob Gibson stand out in ways that Roger Clemens, Tom Seaver, and Jim Palmer do not. Dave Stewart and John Smoltz are perhaps at a level just below the Gibson-Koufax group. Hunter is firmly enshrined in that upper class, the best of the best.

Jim Hunter was born on a farm in Hertford, North Carolina. He was a high school pitching star, ticketed for greatness. The day after helping his prep football team win the state championship, Hunter had his little toe blown off when his brother's shotgun accidentally went off while he was hunting. He recovered, but his bonus baby status among baseball's intelligentsia was over.

Enter Finley, who in his first few years as Kansas City A's owner had this to say of baseball scouts: "What good are they? All they do is sit around all day watching games." So Finley made himself his chief scout. Hearing of Hunter, he investigated, deciding the injury was a blessing (to him) that would allow him to sign a top prospect for cheap rates. Catfish worked the old man for $75,000, still less than he

This sequence of photos shows Catfish Hunter throughout the night that he tossed a perfect game against Minnesota in 1968.

would have gotten if he were fielding bids from the rest of the teams in those predraft days. Then Charlie O. said he needed a nickname. A story was needed.

Hunter told the owner that as a boy he had run away from home, which meant he went fishing for the day, and as a peace offering came home with "a mess of catfish" for supper. After that he was "Catfish" Hunter.

"I did fish a lot as a boy, but I didn't think much of my name," he said in Bill Libby's *Charlie O. and the Angry A's*. "But I also didn't want to cross this man who was spending so much money on me, so I said all right."

Hunter thought the name would not stick, but, largely because of the colorful Monte Moore, it did. He never pitched in the minor leagues and took years to develop into an effective big leaguer. He made the All-Star team in 1967. In 1968 he threw a perfect game against Minnesota, also driving in three runs with a pair of singles. After the game, Finley called him in the clubhouse from La Porte, Indiana, to tell him, "You've just cost me $5,000," a bonus in his contract that the owner doubtless thought would never be paid.

Catfish was a good pitcher in 1969 and 1970, but not great. He gave up a lot of home runs, albeit usually with nobody on base. But he developed. Probably because of adjustments he had made due to the foot injury, he never threw exceptionally hard, but he became a control artist.

"Hunter knows what he's doing on every pitch," said catcher Dave Duncan. "He doesn't have much of a fastball, but he can put everything where he wants it, and everything he throws breaks at a different speed. He keeps the hitters off balance."

Hunter became a 20-game winner in 1971, but his 1972 record (21–7, 2.04 ERA, plus superb performances versus the Tigers and Reds in the postseason) overshadowed his previous efforts. From 1973 to 1975, he was 21–5, 25–12, and 23–14. (But he was with the Yankees in '75, after unexpectedly becoming a free agent when Finley refused to honor his contract after the 1974 season.)

The truth is that Hunter became too expensive for Finley, who realized the pitcher was now so good that he could not afford him. Finley probably figured that breach of contract was cheaper than

DID YOU KNOW . . .

That during the 1973 World Series, Charlie O. Finley moved all of the A's players' wives and family members to seats in the second deck in order to make room for his personal entourage? When the players threatened not to play unless their wives were allowed to sit in their usual seats, Finley relented.

paying the man and that George Steinbrenner would take him off his hands. In that regard, Finley again was on the mark.

Free agency hit that off-season, the result of Curt Flood's Supreme Court challenge to baseball's Reserve Clause four years earlier. The new economics of baseball turned Catfish into a gentleman farmer.

Steinbrenner and the Yankees were one of the few teams with the money to compete for free agents in the 1970s, creating some gloomy predictions, some of which almost came true but, for the most part, eventually worked themselves out.

Catfish had some arm problems after his initial 23-win, 2.58 ERA season in New York, but he recovered to help pitch the Bronx Bombers to the 1978 world championship. His teammate in New York was Reggie Jackson. The two of them earned five world championship rings each. Three of those came against Los Angeles (1974, 1977, and 1978).

TRIVIA

How did Catfish Hunter end up becoming a free agent after the 1974 season?

Answers to the trivia questions are on pages 196–198.

Catfish may well have won 300 games in his career, but the arm problems resurfaced after 1978. He retired with 224 wins and a 3.26 ERA. He was 4–3 in the playoffs and 5–3 in the World Series, but that is misleading. He was brilliant twice versus Detroit in 1972 with no decision, lost the second game of the 1976 Series to Cincinnati despite pitching a fine game, and took a sore-armed loss against L.A. in 1977.

Catfish never let money or New York fame go to his head.

"I don't need a lot of glory," he said, claiming he spent more money feeding his hunting dogs than "my wife and kids. I can tell each dog from the other by the howl. Everybody's got their own kind of music."

Early in Hunter's career, Finley discovered a codicil in Hunter's contract: much of the owner's bonus to the pitcher was actually a loan, buried in boilerplate language. Finley called him before each start demanding payment, threatening to call in the loan. Eventually Catfish earned enough to get the man off his back.

He retired to a 100-acre spread outside Hertford, claiming that "easy livin's made me soft," but this statement was belied by the fact that he helped neighbors harvest peanut crops they needed for survival.

Hunter eventually passed away from Lou Gehrig's disease.

Silent Joe

On a team filled with characters, nicknames, and wild hairstyles, one player stands out for not standing out. Joe Rudi was born to be an Athletic, right there in Modesto, longtime home of the Athletics' Class A California League team, located just a few hours' drive from the friendly confines of the Oakland Coliseum.

The Scandinavian Rudi was one guy without a nickname. Some just called him "Gentleman Joe," which is what he was. He was so fair-skinned and flaxen-haired that when the team grew mustaches for bonus money, his barely came in. He did grow his hair down to his back collar, but it just did not compare to that of his wild and wooly teammates.

Sal Bando looked like a Mob hit man. Reggie Jackson looked like he could take over for the Jackson Five. Dave Duncan looked like he should be protesting the war a few miles up the freeway at Berkeley. Rollie Fingers more resembled the guy who handled cash payoffs at Tammany Hall in the 1880s.

The only other A's player who was as quiet, reserved, and unglamorous was second baseman Dick Green, who was one of the game's great defensive players but could not hit his way out of a paper bag.

The 6'2", 200-pound Rudi came out of Modesto Junior College. A hand injury scared off most scouts, but the genius Finley uncannily picked out another winner, ordering his scout to stick with the lad until he signed.

"From the age of five, all I wanted to be was a player," Rudi once said.

In his mind, his dream came true not in 1967, when he got the call to K.C. for 19 games, but in '66, when he found himself playing for his boyhood favorites, the Modesto A's. It was a team that included Jackson and Duncan and is one of the finest minor league teams ever assembled.

(The locker room at Moana Stadium in Reno once listed all the big leaguers who played in the Cal League, along with many of their records; the league has a long, colorful, and successful history.)

Upon hearing that his exploits drew the attention of Finley, causing Charlie O. to drive from Oakland to Modesto for a look-see, Rudi "was so excited he was coming I hit two homers before he got there. The only thing that was hit after he got there was my hand." Rudi had a career year in Modesto with 24 homers, 85 RBIs, and a .297 average. He struggled to make it in the bigs, getting called up but not particularly impressing anybody until 1970, when he broke through to hit .309. He may not have had that opportunity but for Reggie Jackson simultaneously slumping and feuding with the owner over contract negotiations.

"I owe everything I have to Reggie," Rudi joked.

Reggie certainly owed Joe, too. When they were teammates at Birmingham, Joe and his wife regularly invited Reggie for dinner in the segregated town. The landlady asked him who "the colored guy" was. Joe said it was none of her business.

Rudi was never the main attraction. Monte Moore, who lived in the Central Valley town of Porterville in the off-season, identified with the blue-collar Rudi, but his name, his demeanor, his personality, and his power numbers paled in comparison to larger-than-life teammates.

That said, and guys like Jackson are the first to admit it, Rudi was a key man on the club, the glue offensively and defensively. He hit .305 for the 1972 World Series champs, but his spectacular grab of Denis Menke's near homer at Riverfront Stadium in Game 2 probably was the deciding factor in whether Oakland won or lost that Series.

He hit 22 homers with 99 RBIs in 1974, but it was his home run off Mike Marshall in the fifth game of the

TRIVIA

In Game 4 of the 1974 American League championship series, Oakland won the game, 1–0. How many hits did the team have?

Answers to the trivia questions are on pages 196–198.

World Series that won it, propelling his team to a 3–2 victory. The importance of that home run increases upon retrospection. Had the Dodgers pulled out the 2–2 game, they would have returned to Dodger Stadium with momentum and the pitching to back it up.

Rudi was one of those names fans puzzled over in 1968 and 1969, when the team was first getting established in the San Francisco Bay Area. The Giants were "the team"; National League champions of 1962, contenders every year, they had engaged in death struggles with the Koufax-Drysdale Dodgers; had superstars like Willie Mays, Willie McCovey, and Juan Marichal; and in 1968 finished second behind the defending world champion Cardinals.

Fans reading box scores from spring training or listening to the broadcasts of Monte Moore, Bob Elston, and Red Rush, who handled

Unheralded outfielder Joe Rudi was an All-Star. Here he connects in a 1973 World Series game against the Mets. Photo courtesy of Getty Images.

That prior to the 1974 World Series, several Dodgers players told the press that only two A's—Reggie Jackson and Bert Campaneris—would start for L.A.? "I say we should dispose of those people quickly," Reggie Jackson told Sal Bando. "Buck, that sounds like an excellent idea," Bando replied. Oakland won in five games.

A's games in the early seasons, tried to make sense out of these guys: Rudi, Bando, Campaneris, Nash, Hunter, Aker, Krausse, Odom, Blue.

Then a funny thing happened. The A's got better than the Giants. In 1969, under Hank Bauer, they won 88 games to San Francisco's 90. The next year Oakland won 89 while the Giants won 86. The tide had turned.

In 1971 San Francisco did win the West, but Oakland won their division in the manner of an emerging dynasty. Over the next seasons, the Giants struggled while Oakland grabbed the imagination not just of the Bay's residents, but of a nation.

Most of those players—Rudi, Bando, Hunter, Jackson—were household names by the mid-1970s. Joe Rudi took free-agent gold at California but never became a star in Hollywood's shadow, even though the Angels improved during the years in which Oakland was known as the "Triple A's." Joe played on the Angels' 1979 division champions, a pretty fair ballclub, but was not with them in 1982.

That team, which included the still-great Jackson, lost to Milwaukee after blowing a 2–0 lead in the best-of-five series, but its potent offense is still regarded as one of the best ever, a baseball version of Dan Fouts's Chargers of the same period.

Rudi came back to Oakland in 1982, but his skills were not the same.

"It's Hold 'Em Rollie Fingers Time"

Rollie Fingers, like so many before and since, came out of the sun-splashed fields of Southern California to carve out a niche for himself in baseball history. He was considered the top high school pitching prospect of 1964 (the injured Hunter now thought to be a caution). Fingers pitched the Rancho Cucamonga American Legion team to the national championship, then signed on with the A's franchise.

Fingers had mixed success in the minor leagues. He was part of the great 1966 Modesto team, posting an 11–6 record with a 2.77 earned-run average, but after breaking in with Oakland in 1968, he experienced four inconsistent years. The 6'4" right-hander had all the talent in the world: he threw hard, he had a wicked slider, and he was imposing in every way. His mechanics were excellent, his stuff overpowering.

It was assumed that he would be a starting pitcher. When he came up, the best pitchers were starters. The bullpen was left to secondary guys or over-the-hill veterans. Fingers never thrived as a starter.

In 1972 he was moved to the bullpen and enjoyed immediate success. He would come into a game with men all over the bases, the crowd going crazy, threat hanging in the air like palpable danger; then he would calmly strike out a couple of dangerous hitters to save the day.

"Rollie was too dumb to know any better," teammate Rick Monday said, actually meaning it as a compliment. "He didn't know any better, guys all over the sacks, 3–2 count, he'd throw a 'yak slider' on the outside black for strike three. Other pitchers would be too afraid to walk the guy and groove one that would get hit."

Rollie changed the whole nature of relief pitching, but his own metamorphosis paralleled the game's. He went from starter to relief pitcher, which in 1972 could mean middle, set-up, closer—or all three. It was not unusual to see Ken Holtzman pitch five and give way to Rollie for four!

Sometimes Rollie "vultured" wins, giving up the tying run, then settling down to collect the victory when the A's scored to go ahead. He got lazy sometimes, letting opponents fill the bases before settling into a groove. He blew a few games here and there, but when the clutch was on

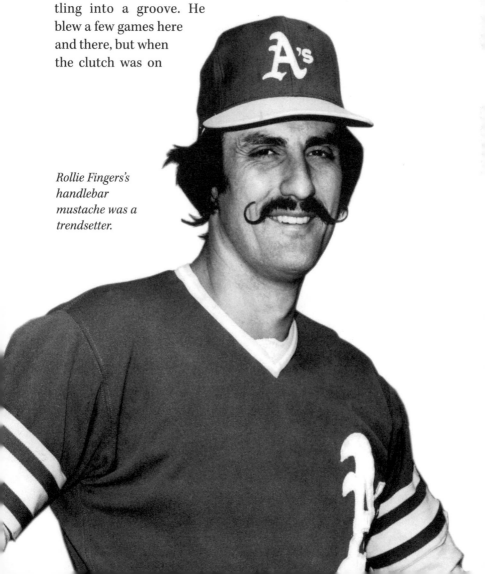

Rollie Fingers's handlebar mustache was a trendsetter.

in the playoffs or World Series, with very few exceptions, Fingers was outstanding.

With Rollie on the hill with a one-run lead in the ninth, which seemed to characterize 90 percent of Oakland's wins (and virtually all their postseason victories) in the 1970s, Monte Moore would announce, "It's hold 'em Rollie Fingers time."

He left Johnny Bench literally holding his bat in the 1972 Series, working with Dick Williams and Gene Tenace to feign an intentional walk before throwing one of those "yak sliders" for a strikeout. Bench just stared out at Fingers, half flabbergasted, half in awe.

When Whitey Herzog said Rollie was the "most valuable player in the league," it seemed incongruous. Mike Marshall of Los Angeles was the first reliever to win the Cy Young Award, but Rollie took that a step further, winning the Cy Young and MVP awards at Milwaukee in 1981. Because of the way he was used, Rollie never saved as many games in Oakland as other great relievers. His Oakland ERAs were tremendous: 2.51 (1972), 1.91 (1973), 2.65 (1974), 2.98 (1975), and 2.47 (1976).

Eventually, baseball's economics forced Oakland to part with Rollie and the rest of his mates after the 1976 campaign. At San

TOP 10

All-Time Saves Leaders (As of 2006)

1.	Trevor Hoffman	482
2.	Lee Smith	478
3.	John Franco	424
4.	Mariano Rivera	413
5.	**Dennis Eckersley**	390
6.	Jeff Reardon	367
7.	Randy Myers	347
8.	**Rollie Fingers**	341
9.	John Wetteland	330
10.	Roberto Hernandez	326

Players shown in bold played for the A's at some point during their careers.

DID YOU KNOW . . . That Rick Monday once got a phone call from Charlie O. Finley to invest in a stock "right now. Not tomorrow, not in two hours, right now!"? Finley promised a written guarantee that Monday's $30,000 investment would be paid back if he lost it, so he came up with the dough. A few days later Finley called to say, "Call your stock broker. Get out, NOW! RIGHT NOW!" Monday did, at a substantial profit. "Old Charlie had some serious insider trading going on. God only knows how many SEC violations he committed," Monday said in a 1999 interview at Dodger Stadium.

Diego and Milwaukee, used in the closer's role that he defined, Rollie was just as spectacular, if not more, than he had been in Oakland. He helped pitch Milwaukee to the 1982 American League pennant and retired after 1985 with a then-major-league-record 341 saves and a 2.90 ERA in 1,701 innings (1968–1985). Rollie was elected to Cooperstown in 1992.

The specialty he perfected paved the way for the likes of Goose Gossage, Bruce Sutter, Lee Smith, Dennis Eckersley, and Mariano Rivera, among others. Rivera approaches Fingers as a big-game closer, a "lights out" stopper, but when looking at the big picture, Fingers may be the greatest relief pitcher the game has ever known.

Billy Ball

Then there was Billy Martin: scrappy, white trash, alcoholic; drinking pal of Mickey Mantle, Whitey Ford, and Art Fowler; supercompetitive New York icon; mercenary manager; and politically incorrect cautionary tale.

Billy, number one in your program and the number one of many in their hearts, is often associated with New York, where of course he helped lead the Yankees to no less than five World Series titles from 1950 to 1956. He was traded, playing everywhere and then managing everywhere. People who move from one job to another—for instance, a newspaper editor who takes a job at a flagging paper, rights the ship, wears out his welcome, and moves on, only to repeat the act over and over—would become known as the "Billy Martin of newspaper editors," or the "Billy Martin of casino GMs," or the "Billy Martin of basketball" (read: Larry Brown), whatever the case may be.

Aside from his New York persona, however, Billy is as associated with East Bay baseball as much as anything else. First, he starred at Berkeley High School. Second, he earned his spurs playing under Casey Stengel and the Oakland Oaks of the Pacific Coast League. That association was the break he needed to get to the bigs when Casey took over the Yankees.

Last, but not least, Billy revived (or some might say *created*) baseball excitement as manager of the A's in the early 1980s. He was spectacular, the team was a big hit, but like everything he touched in his personal and professional life, it all fell apart. Billy always self-destructed. In Oakland his wrecking ball came in the form of an observation that the team was "run by a bunch of Jews." Ouch.

Billy grew up tough and hard on the playing fields of west Berkeley. He lacked size, speed, strength, a great arm, or any of the accoutrements of baseball greatness. He made up for it with a scrappy attitude, a desire to beat anybody standing in his way. It carried him to the Yankees, where he saved a World Series game with the bases loaded by racing about two miles to grab a pop fly that nobody else seemingly wanted any part of.

Country boy Mickey Mantle, smarting from impolite press comparisons with Joe DiMaggio, needed somebody to go drinkin' with. Billy was happy to oblige. Whitey Ford, who only pitched every fourth or fifth day and so had the time, made sure they did it right. By 1957, after a celebrated tête-à-tête at the Copa, this act was an embarrassment. Because Ford and Mantle were superstars, it was Billy who got traded to Kansas City. They would have to drink in the off-season, usually at Mantle's Texas ranch where they would go "hunting."

Martin eventually got into managing. Minnesota: division champs. Detroit: division champs. Texas: from losers to contenders. In each case, general managers, players, and press: smarting from run-ins with man-child Billy. Then George Steinbrenner hired him in New York. What a move! Billy immediately restored New York to glory with the 1977 world championship. With the Yankees floundering the following season, Martin resigned and told reporters, referring to his run-ins with Reggie Jackson and Steinbrenner: "They deserve each other. One's a born liar, and the other's convicted." (This comment referred to Steinbrenner's conviction for illegal campaign contributions to Richard Nixon in 1972.) Good-bye, Billy. It was just a plot twist to the whole "Bronx Zoo" soap opera when Billy was invited back to manage *in two years,* while Bob Lemon handled the rest of the seemingly play-out-the-season 1978 chores. (In July they were 14 games back.) Except Lemon took New York all the way to a repeat Series title.

In 1979, a year earlier than planned, Billy came back, but second acts never were or would be his forte. It seemed to be over. Meanwhile, Charlie O. was cutting his losses, selling the so-called Triple A's to whoever would take them off his hands. The franchise seemed to be bound for its fourth city since 1954. In 1980 the A's were purchased by the Haas group of the Levi Strauss jeans empire. That season, Billy came on as manager.

Almost as if by miracle, Martin turned the team around from 54–108 to 83–79. Mike Norris was 22–9 with a 2.54 ERA. Rick Langford was 19–12 with a 3.26 ERA. Tony Armas hit 35 homers with 109 RBIs. Rickey Henderson emerged as a star. Attendance picked up.

Oakland's style was called "Billy Ball." It meant stolen bases, bunts, squeeze plays, and first-and-third double steals. It was perfect for Henderson.

"Billy was my favorite manager," he stated.

Martin also was old school when it came to using his pitchers. Bullpen?

"I don't need no stinkin' bullpen," he might as well have said.

His guys went nine. When all his promising pitchers—Norris, Langford, Matt Keough, Steve McCatty, and Brian Kingman—flamed out early in their careers, Martin's overuse of them was blamed, with plenty of justification.

Nobody questioned him in 1981, however. The team entered the season with enormous expectations. After winning the first 11

After several down years, the hiring of Bay Area native Billy Martin signaled revival and controversy in Oakland.

By the NUMBERS

9—The number of times Billy Martin was hired and fired: Twins (1969), Tigers (1971–1973), Rangers (1973–1975), Yankees (1975–1978), Yankees (1979), A's (1980–1982), Yankees (1983), Yankees (1985), and Yankees (1988).

games of the season, Oakland was the new baseball capital of the world. The Coliseum was filled to overflowing, excitement over Billy Ball at a fever pitch. It was one of the greatest franchise turnarounds in the game's history. It saved baseball in Oakland.

In a strike-shortened season, the A's won the West behind Norris, McCatty, Langford, and Keough. In April and May 1981, the A's were airtight. Scoring on them was like trying to throw hamburger through a brick wall.

Henderson became a genuine superstar. He had broken Ty Cobb's league record for stolen bases, finishing with 100 in 1980, and led the AL with 56 in 1981 to go with a .319 average.

By season's end, though, there were signs of the team's unraveling. The pitching staff was worn thin, their weaknesses exposed in a three-game playoff sweep by the Yankees. In 1982 high hopes were quickly dashed in a brutal 68–94 campaign.

Billy's drinking became a public embarrassment. He reportedly was drunk at the park, drunk during games, drunk most of the time. His drinking buddy was pitching coach Art Fowler, an old Yankees pal. Art

TRIVIA

What famous rap star was the "general manager" of the A's while still a teenager in the late 1970s?

Answers to the trivia questions are on pages 196–198.

did little coaching. The starters just took the ball and made complete games. Art could drink Billy under the table, which was the problem, because Billy let him.

With failure came recriminations, and with blame getting tossed around, Billy made his infamous "too many Jews" remark, getting himself tossed in the process. Steinbrenner brought him back, but the act was worn thin. Eventually, Billy met a predictable demise: death in a drunk-driving car crash.

Completing What They Started

Baseball has changed drastically over the years. Nineteen sixty-eight is remembered as the "Year of the Pitcher." The combined earned-run average of both major leagues was below 3.00. Carl Yastrzemski of Boston won the American League batting title at .301. He was the only .300 hitter in the league.

The All-Star Game in Houston was won by the Nationals, 1–0. Don Drysdale of Los Angeles broke Walter Johnson's all-time consecutive scoreless innings record with 58. There were five no-hitters thrown. Gaylord Perry of the Giants and Ray Washburn of the Cardinals threw no-no's on consecutive days at Candlestick Park against each other's teams. Catfish Hunter of the A's tossed a perfect game.

The MVP of both leagues was a pitcher. In the American League, Detroit's Denny McLain was baseball's last 30-game winner, but his performance was overshadowed, if one can believe it, by St. Louis's Bob Gibson, the NL Most Valuable Player and Cy Young Award winner. Gibby threatened Johnson's scoreless innings streak before Drysdale, finally giving up a run after 48 straight zeros. His 1.12 earned-run average came on the strength of 13 shutouts.

Mickey Lolich was the pitching hero of the World Series, winning three games to capture the MVP trophy for the champion Tigers. As great as pitching performances were in 1968, there were no great relievers who stood out. It was an era of starting pitchers who pitched complete games.

With attendance down, baseball decided they needed more runs and more excitement. They lowered the mound in 1969, then the American League brought in the designated hitter a few years later.

San Francisco native Mike Norris was a 22-game winner in 1980 but may have been overused by Billy Martin. Photo courtesy of Getty Images.

DID YOU KNOW ... That the city of Oakland once tried to put on a promotion combining the A's and the Raiders? When Raiders coach John Madden heard they were planning to bring the mule, Charlie O., to the Coliseum for a football game, he said, "Hell no, they're not bringing in any mules."

Offense picked up. Managers like Sparky Anderson of the Reds, Dick Williams of the A's, and even the old-school Walt Alston of the Dodgers created new strategies based on strong bullpens. The roles of the set-up man and the closer were redefined by Rollie Fingers, Goose Gossage, and Bruce Sutter.

By the late 1970s, championship teams got there on the strength of great relievers. In analyzing why the Baltimore Orioles won only one World Series between 1969 and 1979, despite having the best starting pitching in the game throughout much of that era, it becomes apparent they lost to lesser teams because they lacked a dominant closer.

Every year, teams won world championships with guys like Fingers, Gossage, Darold Knowles, Rawly Eastwick, Kent Tekulve, Tug McGraw, and Steve Howe.

Then, along came Billy Martin and his starting pitchers. In 1980 the A's threw—this is not a typo—*94 complete games!* Mike Norris was 22–9 with a 2.54 earned-run average. Norris, Matt Keough (16–13, 2.92 ERA), Steve McCatty (14–14, 3.85), and Rick Langford (19–12, 3.26 ERA) each pitched 14-inning complete games. They all won their games except McCatty, a 2–1 loser.

Langford led the league with 28 complete games in 1980. Twenty-two of them were consecutive. He was 12–10 in 1981, a strike-shortened year in which the A's won the West, with 18 complete games.

In 1981 Norris was 12–9 with a 3.75 ERA. McCatty threw 16 complete games in a 14–7 campaign to go with a 2.32 earned-run average. Keough was 10–6 with a 3.41 ERA.

Why did Martin emphasize complete games so much? For one, the A's had no great relief pitchers. In New York Martin had Sparky Lyle, whom he had gone to often enough in the world championship 1977 season that Lyle won the Cy Young Award. Goose Gossage replaced Lyle, and of course Bob Lemon replaced Billy, but Martin did have Gossage in 1978 (before Martin resigned) and 1979 (before he was fired).

When he was asked about it, Martin just said that he was making do with what he had at his disposal. Langford, Norris, McCatty, and Keough pitching the eighth and ninth innings of games were more effective, to Billy's way of thinking, than whatever he had in the bullpen.

Martin was of course an old school baseball man who played on Yankees teams with great pitching. The three New York teams of his era, the 1950s, all featured guys who regularly went the distance: Whitey Ford, Allie Reynolds, Eddie Lopat, and Vic Raschi of the Yankees; Don Newcombe and Carl Erskine of Brooklyn; and Sal Maglie and Jim Hearn of the Giants.

It was all very exciting, but of course Oakland's complete-game pitching staff made it that way by not just finishing what they started, but by winning, too. However, it is difficult to look at all those young arms, so effective for just a few seasons, then flaming out, without placing blame on Martin for burning them out, mentally and physically.

This of course brings up an age-old baseball argument, because for decades pitchers regularly did throw complete games. Wilcy Moore was perhaps baseball's first star relief pitcher when he was 19–7 with a 2.28 ERA for the "all-time greatest" 1927 Yankees. But he still started 12 games, completing six in that, his rookie year. He was 13–3 with 13 saves out of the pen.

Relief pitchers tended to be oddities. Ryne Duren of the Yankees came into games squinting at home plate out of glasses said to look like the caps of Coke bottles. His first warm-up would be a 100-mile-per-hour heater into the backstop, conveying the message to the upcoming hitter that to dig in could mean a trip to the hospital. Duren had flashes of brilliance but not a long career.

Elroy Face once won 18 games out of the bullpen. He saved 24 for the 1960 world champion Pirates. Dick "the Monster" Radatz was a 6–7 hardballer for Boston in the 1960s. He was one of the first conventionally used (by modern standards) relievers.

The Dodgers established many of the "rules" for relieving in the 1960s when Walt Alston went to Phil Regan and Ron Perranoski to

DID YOU KNOW... That A's pitcher Mike Norris grew up in San Francisco, where he played on the well-regarded Ellis Brooks Chevrolet semipro team that plays on Sundays at Big Rec in Golden Gate Park?

save games for Sandy Koufax, Don Drysdale, and Claude Osteen, but even Regan was something different. He was nicknamed "the Vulture" for his habit of letting the tying run score, then getting the win when L.A. would score to win it in the ninth. He was one of those relievers who looked first to his win-loss record, not his save totals.

The 1969 Amazin' Mets established the five-man rotation under Manager Gil Hodges. When they won the World Series featuring a strong starting staff (Tom Seaver, Jerry Koosman) combined with set-up men (including Nolan Ryan) and a closer (Tug McGraw), baseball sat up and took notice.

The debate over complete games went on throughout the 1970s. Sparky Anderson was nicknamed "Captain Hook" for using so many relievers. After Martin's tenure in Oakland, an explosion of excellent relievers like Lee Smith and Dennis Eckersley came on the scene. The overriding conventional wisdom has been to limit pitch counts before giving way to a structured bullpen made up of set-up men and closers, all of whom follow their defined roles with little deviation.

An example of why this is thought to be the only recipe for success is said to be in Atlanta, where for 16 years the Braves have featured great starters but often struggle to complement them with equally great closers. Consequently, they have won division after division but only one World Series and have lost most of their play-offs year after year.

Hot Dog

"Yes, I am a hot dog.... Ever hear of a hot dog who couldn't play?"

Thus opens *Off Base: Confessions of a Thief* by Rickey Henderson and John Shea. The term *hot dog* perfectly suited Henderson, one of the greatest baseball players of all time, a sure Hall of Famer if and when he ever actually retires, and the greatest base stealer the game has ever known.

Henderson grew up in the shadow of the A's, on the Oakland-Berkeley border. Life was rough in the inner city.

"I knew a lot of guys better than me in sports," he wrote in his autobiography, "but I avoided drugs. I never put anything up my nose or smoked anything. I wanted to enjoy life."

Henderson starred in four sports at Oakland Tech High, but the football team was awful going into his junior year. Then Henderson blossomed, and his team did, too, beating rival Oakland High en route to a winning record. Henderson was a 1,000-yard rusher in his senior year, with football scholarship offers from USC, UCLA, Arizona State, and other major programs.

Henderson was part of the great Oakland–East Bay sports tradition. Many people talk about the golden age of San Francisco prep baseball, the roughly 30 years between the 1920s and early 1950s, and of course Southern California has always been the home of superathletes. But the East Bay has probably produced as many athletic heroes in a relatively smaller population as any other place in the country.

There was Billy Martin and John Lambert of Berkeley; Willie Stargell, Dontrelle Willis, and Jimmy Rollins of Alameda Encinal;

When Rickey Henderson broke Lou Brock's all-time career stolen-base record in 1991, he picked up the bag and announced, Muhammad Ali–style, "I am the greatest...of all time."

Frank Robinson, Vada Pinson, and Joe Morgan of Oakland Castlemont; Jackie Jensen of Oakland High; Bill Russell of McClymonds; Dave Stewart of Oakland St. Elizabeth's; Jason Kidd of Alameda St. Joseph's; Gino Torretta of Pinole Valley; and Dennis Eckersley of Fremont Irvington, just to name a few. Oakland Tech boasted Curt Flood and Henderson, but Tech produced more than just athletes: Black Panther leader Huey Newton and actor Clint Eastwood were also Tech graduates.

In *Off Base*, the chapter describing Rickey's prep football exploits is titled "The Next O.J. Simpson," but Henderson's first love was baseball. He signed with the Oakland A's and quickly ascended to the major leagues. In 1982 Henderson broke Lou Brock's single-season record for stolen bases with 130, "but I could have had more," he stated.

Henderson starred on the successful Billy Ball teams of the early 1980s. Manager Billy Martin, a feisty character, managed to lead the team to winning seasons in 1980 and 1981. These were pivotal years in A's history, coming on the heels of Finley's sale of his so-called Triple A's (as in players of Triple A minor league quality) to the Haas group. The Haas ownership built up the fan base with goodwill, on the strength of Martin's exciting brand of baseball. Nobody embodied that better than Rickey Henderson.

However, the relationship between Martin and his bosses soured, the team dropped out of contention, and Henderson found himself with the New York Yankees. He is not as well remembered in New York as he might be, since those were not championship years, but he performed brilliantly as usual.

In the late 1980s, Oakland developed one of the great dynasties of all time, but something was missing. In 1988 the team was heavily favored but lost to the Los Angeles Dodgers in five games in the World Series. In 1989 they were rolling again when they picked up Henderson about a third of the way into the season. Rickey exploded, putting on one of the most spectacular postseason displays ever as the A's powered past Toronto.

TRIVIA

How many championship teams have been produced in the East Bay?

Answers to the trivia questions are on pages 196–198.

In 1990 he earned American League MVP honors, hitting .325 with 28 home runs, 65 stolen bases, and 119 runs scored.

"If I didn't get this one, I don't know what I would have done," he wrote in his autobiography, referring to "close-but-no-cigar" finishes for the award in 1981 and 1985. In 1991 Henderson broke another of Brock's cherished records, passing him to become the all-time base-stealing leader with 939. Afterward, Henderson held the base aloft and announced, Ali-like through the microphone brought out for the ceremony, "I am now the greatest."

In addition to being the best base stealer ever, Henderson is considered the greatest leadoff hitter of them all and the best leadoff home-run hitter ever.

The "Bash Brothers"

The old Connie Mack phenomenon of feast or famine continued. In Kansas City, it was all famine: an embarrassing series of "trades" of young A's for Yankees cash. In Oakland it was feast time—in a big way. But the fall from grace between 1977 and 1979 was one of the hardest crashes the game has ever known.

Then came Billy Ball, but to quote John Madden, "it's a bluff." Two exciting years (1980 and 1981) divide the terrible late 1970s from the desultory mid-1980s. But despite Billy's fall from grace, Oakland invested in their farm system under the Haas ownership. In 1982 *Baseball America* named the A's "Organization of the Year." Every one of their minor league teams, from Triple A to the Rookie League, finished in first place. Out of this crop came strong arms, speed, and power. Furthermore, talent was available for key trades. Dave Wilder, a promising outfielder, went to the Cubs for Dennis Eckersley. The new brain trust, consisting of Walt Jocketty and Sandy Alderson, made shrewd moves, such as the signing of Dave Stewart, a failure in Los Angeles who had been released after a short stint with Philadelphia.

In 1986 Jose Canseco came up to the big leagues. In 1987 he was joined by first baseman Mark McGwire. They became a home-run-hitting duo reminiscent of Willie Mays and Willie McCovey or Hank Aaron and Eddie Mathews. Canseco and McGwire embodied the success of the late-1980s A's, one of the most talented teams ever assembled. They came to be known as the "Bash Brothers," a symbolic description of two star-crossed players on a star-crossed team.

It all seemed pretty innocent in those halcyon days. In 1987 Oakland struggled to reach the .500 level, but Stewart came into his own with a 20–13 record. McGwire broke all rookie records with 49 home runs, but the team could not overcome its old nemesis, the Minnesota Twins. The Twins were then playing in the infernal Hubert Humphrey Metrodome.

"How could they name such a terrible stadium after a great politician like Hubert Humphrey?" Billy Martin said (revealing his voting sentiments) when the place opened.

It was a house of horrors for Oakland, as well as the St. Louis Cardinals, who lost four games and the World Series there to the Twins in 1987. But in 1988, Oakland came out loaded for bear.

Manager Tony La Russa grew up in Tampa, Florida, with Lou Piniella. A bonus baby, La Russa failed in a brief big-league career with the A's. After becoming an attorney, he returned to baseball, managing the 1983 White Sox to a division title before getting fired. Hired in Oakland, he used his education and all-around cerebral skills to build a better team. He and pitching coach Dave Duncan employed computers to gain the edge. It was well documented in George Will's *Men at Work.*

Dave Parker, a big star in Pittsburgh, was acquired from Cincinnati in a huge off-season pickup. Dave Henderson, who hit two clutch homers for Boston in the 1986 postseason, came over. Relief pitcher Jay Howell was traded to Los Angeles in a controversial move for Bob Welch. Howell was an All-Star. Welch, after a promising start that included a huge 1978 World Series K of Reggie Jackson, had descended into alcoholism, although he had taken to recovery.

Oakland was a juggernaut. They started hot and never left off, powering their way to an MLB-best 104–58 mark. Stewart was 21–12 with a 3.23 ERA. Welch was 17–9 with a 3.64 ERA. Storm Davis was 16–7. The middle relief of Gene Nelson, Todd Burns, Rick Honeycutt, Eric Plunk, and Greg Cadaret was nothing less than extraordinary. Then there was Eckersley: 45 saves, a 2.35 earned-run average, total dominance.

Catcher Terry Steinbach was the MVP of the All-Star Game. First baseman McGwire hit 32 home runs. Rookie shortstop Walt Weiss was a defensive star. Reliable veteran third baseman Carney Lansford, a Santa Clara Wilcox star, returned to the Bay Area after years in Anaheim. Dave "Hendu" Henderson finally realized his potential with 24 knocks, 94 runs batted in, and a .304 average. Parker was a presence in the middle of the lineup. Then there was Jose.

The self-described "greatest player in the world," Canseco was just that in '88 when he hit 42 home runs and became baseball's first "40/40 man"—40 homers and 40 stolen bases. He hit .307, knocked in 124 runs, and earned MVP honors.

For several years in the late 1980s and early 1990s, the "Bash Brothers," Mark McGwire (left) and Jose Canseco, were a devastating power combo.

All-1980s A's Team

Position	Name
Right-Handed Pitcher	Dave Stewart
Right-Handed Pitcher	Bob Welch
Right-Handed Pitcher	Rick Langford
Right-Handed Pitcher	Mike Norris
Relief Pitcher	Dennis Eckersley
Catcher	Terry Steinbach
First Baseman	Mark McGwire
Second Baseman	Tony Phillips
Third Baseman	Carney Lansford
Shortstop	Walt Weiss
Outfielder	Rickey Henderson
Outfielder	Dave Henderson
Outfielder	Jose Canseco
Manager	Tony La Russa

The playoffs pitted Oakland against Boston. After Oakland won the opener, Boston's Roger Clemens was staked to a 2–0 lead at Fenway Park, but a Red Sox win was not to be. The A's came back on the Cy Young Award winner, securing victory and momentum, which carried them to a 4–0 sweep at Oakland.

Los Angeles was their World Series opponent, but this was not the arrogant crew Oakland had beaten 14 years earlier. Lasorda was their manager, and he was no more humble, but the Dodgers were underdogs who took to the role.

The Mets were the class of the National League. When they rallied in the ninth of the NLCS opener to win after Orel Hershiser blew them away for eight scoreless innings, it was seemingly over, but L.A. scrapped back. Orel shut them out in Game 7 to send the World Series back to Dodger Stadium for another all-California Series, 14 years after the first one and a decade since they lost to the Reggie-Catfish '78 Yankees.

Records indicate the A's were big favorites. L.A. had little talent and less of a chance. This is revisionism. On paper, the A's looked superior. They were favored and should have won, but the David and Goliath comparisons do not quite hold up. What *was* stunning was the fact that Los Angeles dismantled the Oakland A's in five games.

Lasorda's team was 94–67. They had Kirk Gibson, a former Michigan State football star who hit 25 homers and won the league MVP award. Their lineup was indeed lacking the A's power, but they scrapped, had some speed, and played good defense. But it was the old Mack adage that "pitching is 90 percent of baseball," especially in a short series, that rung true and was in fact a predictor before the first game.

Tim Leary (17–11) and Tim Belcher (12–6) threw hard and were nobody's pushovers. Howell (2.08, 21 saves) made the Welch trade agreeable for both sides. But L.A.'s great equalizer was Hershiser. God touched him that year. Take any great pitcher from any year: Christy Mathewson (1905), "Smoky Joe" Wood (1912), Walter Johnson (1913), Lefty Grove (1931), Bob Gibson and Denny McLain (1968), Tom Seaver (1969), Ron Guidry (1978), and you'll find that none has ever been better than Orel in 1988, at least not in the second half of that season.

His pitches looked like Moses's staff when he tells the Pharaoh Ramses to set his people free. They were not baseballs thrown by a human hand, they were dancing snakes with fiery tails. No human being holding a bat could be expected to hit such things. None did.

Fifty-nine scoreless innings to close the season, breaking Don Drysdale's record of 58 straight shutout innings. The Mets, a bunch of sluggers, touched him not. He was not scheduled to pitch against the A's until Game 2 at Dodger Stadium. The A's just figured he would win two games and they would have to beat the other guys. If Game 1 got away from Oakland, then Orel would win

TRIVIA

When the Haas ownership group took over the A's from Charlie O. Finley, attendance picked up rapidly, and by the late 1980s they were considered a model franchise, a business success, and a major box-office draw at home and on the road. What marketing guru is given much of the credit for the public relations success of the A's?

Answers to the trivia questions are on pages 196–198.

That when Jose Canseco came up to the big leagues, he was ill at ease under the media, so the A's hired Reggie Jackson, then nearing the end of his career, as Canseco's PR advisor?

and the A's would suddenly be looking at a 2–0 deficit. When this happened, all bets were off. A faster closing than the one predicted by Zero Mostel in *The Producers*.

In the opener, the Dodgers jumped out to a 2–0 lead, but Canseco answered with a grand slam in the second, and form held until the scrappy Dogs made it 4–3 going into the ninth. In: Eck. Therefore: ballgame. Or so it seemed. With two outs Eck faced a former Athletic named Mike Davis, who had not done a darn thing since hitting a triple off Buddy Biancalana to give San Diego Hoover a 6–5 win over Larkspur Redwood, ending Redwood's unbeaten streak in 1977!

For some reason, Eck treated him with the respect he would accord Carl Yastrzemski in his prime. Four wide ones, tying run on, winning run coming up. Kirk Gibson, injured, gimpy—*no way he plays!*—limps to home plate. Forget the script; this is not in the script. It was ridiculous. *Rewrite it.* The guy was not even in the dugout; he was prowling around the outer corridors, away from his team, injured, unable to play, *pissed!*

Lasorda puts him in. Eck dominates him. Gibson takes a couple of the worst flails imaginable but gets a nick to stay alive. Eck throws a backdoor slider. Gibby, with one leg (literally, his back leg is in the air) and with one hand (actually), waves his bat like Belinda the Good Witch of the North. The swing looked to generate enough power to pop one to Weiss.

The Holy Spirit was in that bat, though, and then in the ball. No other way to explain how the *pelota* jumped off that bat and traveled over the right-field fence for a game-winning home run.

On Sunday Hershiser shoved the bat so far up Oakland's keisters they could not walk for a week, which explains why they went down after that like the Turks at Aqaba. Orel blew 'em away in Game 5, and it was over. Series done.

Jose

What more is there to be said about Jose Canseco? He was about 5'11", 185 pounds as an 18-year-old kid out of Miami's Coral Park High School.

Four years after he played at Idaho Falls, Idaho, of the Pioneer League, he was *Baseball America*'s reigning Minor League Player of the Year, a surefire major league star. His home-run totals from 1982 to 1985 are two ('82), 14 ('83), 15 ('84), and 41 ('85, which includes a September call-up to Oakland). What was going on there?

Jose is "credited" with bringing steroids into baseball, but anybody who ever looked at Brian Downing of the Angels in the late 1970s might suspect that the juice was around before Canseco. When did Jose start doing it? The fans were on him about it as early as 1988, when people started noticing that the A's looked more like a football team than a baseball team.

He claims to have introduced McGwire to it, injecting steroids via a needle into Mark's buttocks in an Oakland Coliseum bathroom stall. In 1991 the Cal Bears played the A's in an exhibition game at the Coliseum. During batting practice before the game, Cal's hopefuls all crowded around like kids at the carnival to see Canseco hit long bombs, then roll up his sleeves, exposing humongous biceps in acts of blatant machismo with Dave Henderson and others.

Jose did 'roids as much to make himself irresistible to the ladies as to make himself a baseball star. He had it goin' on. His wives and girlfriends over the years were always top-of-the-line. His last spouse graced *Playboy* in 2005 and there were no letters of complaint. He dated Madonna when the A's traveled to New York, but she could not handle a star bigger than she was.

But Jose had a clown side to him. He had some defensive skills when he came up but did not work at it. His lack of glove tools was exemplified by an easy fly ball that bounced off his head over the fence for a home run. In a game that was well decided, he pitched an inning and managed to hurt his arm so badly he was out for the season. The steroids caused numerous strange injuries: back spasms, arm problems, tendon tweaks.

He was the furthest guy from a team player, which caused endless pain for La Russa. He got pulled midgame in 1992, traded to Texas in a "good riddance" move. But Jose was a major star in Oakland. He played on three straight American League champions, although there is some validity to the argument that had he been a more complete player—better defensively, less selfish, more of a

Jose Canseco may well have started the steroid era in baseball. He liked to strike "muscle" poses, flexing his biceps in macho displays during batting practice.

go-to guy in the clutch—his team might have won three world championships instead of one.

He played for half the American League. He was a designated hitter, so the National League was out. But nobody can deny that he could hit.

TRIVIA

When Jose Canseco broke into the major leagues, what nickname was originally given to him?

Answers to the trivia questions are on pages 196–198.

Sure, it was the steroids, but the man hit laser beams everywhere he went. Jose finally retired shy of the 500 home runs that experts say "ensure" Hall of Fame induction. Many breathed a sigh of relief because they did not want to see him enshrined, for many reasons. The most obvious one became more obvious when he revealed in 2005's *Juiced* just how 'roided he and most of the game's biggest sluggers were in the 1990s and 2000s.

In an ironic twist of fate, the book was Jose's last laugh. His lifetime stats are perilously close to Hall-worthy, but considering his defensive liabilities, not enough to get him in. He does not have the personality or the temperament to be a manager or coach, so his de facto blackballing meant the bridges he burned had already been set afire by others.

His fellow players called him a liar, but oddly Jose had the look of truth to him, somehow managing to sound like Whittaker Chambers withstanding the establishment's beating of him during the Alger Hiss affair. As events developed—McGwire looking like a deer caught in headlights when asked about steroids, Rafael Palmeiro testing positive after a Clintonian denial—Jose had the last laugh, a best seller and millions in profits.

Only in America.

DID YOU KNOW . . . That Bob Nightengale of *The Sporting News* once wrote of Jose Canseco that, "Here was Michael Jordan, Steve Young, and Dennis Rodman all rolled into one. He was a Hollywood star, and the playing field simply was his stage"?

October 1989

Considering what we now know about Jose Canseco and Mark McGwire, the fact that their moment of ultimate glory—the 1989 world championship—was a star-crossed affair is fittingly ironic.

On paper, the 1989 A's are one of the most powerful teams ever. They are part of a three-year run (plus a four-out-of-five-year period) that could have rivaled the best in the game's history but instead fell short.

Oakland came off their 1988 World Series loss to Los Angeles bound and determined to right that wrong. They started off with a pitching staff rivaling the Big Three of early 1970s fame: Dave Stewart (21–9, 3.32), Mike Moore (19–11, 2.61), Bob Welch (17–8), Storm Davis (19–7), middle relievers Gene Nelson and Rick Honeycutt, and closer Dennis Eckersley (33 saves, 1.56).

It was the best of times and, while certainly not the worst of times, a portent of tougher times. The first sign came in the form of Canseco's injuries, which kept him to only 65 games. It was always something: his back, his foot, his elbow, his tendons. What it was, was steroids, which cause these things to happen. His relationship with his manager also frayed in 1989.

"After his 40/40 year, he got an awful lot of attention and started to make some serious money," La Russa said in Glenn Dickey's *Champions.* "As happens to so many young guys when they get attention, their values go sideways. You could see it. I had conversations with Jose, telling him he was losing track of what it's all about."

After one game in which Canseco swung for the fences with a man on third and a single would have won it, La Russa confronted the slugger only to be told, "I'm an entertainer. People would rather

When Oakland swept San Francisco in the 1989 Earthquake Series, it was a return to glory, but ultimately Manager Tony La Russa's club did not meet its potential.

TOP 10

A's Pitchers

1. Lefty Grove
2. Eddie Plank
3. Catfish Hunter
4. Rube Waddell
5. Chief Bender
6. Dennis Eckersley
7. Rollie Fingers
8. Vida Blue
9. Dave Stewart
10. Barry Zito

see me take three big swings, maybe hit one out of the park, maybe strike out, than just hit a single."

La Russa is an educated, erudite fellow, but Canseco made his blood boil over.

Then there was the return of Rickey Henderson via a blockbuster June trade with the Yankees. Henderson indeed was spectacular and helped lead Oakland to the promised land, but he was another thorn in the side of a manager struggling to control a team of superstars.

"What Rickey needed wasn't always what the club needed," said La Russa. "That really only happened a few times, but every time it did, it seemed to become public, so it seemed bigger than it was. Rickey was always very much influenced by those around him...."

Rickey's 77 stolen bases led the league, as did his 126 walks and 113 runs scored (tied). McGwire hit 33 home runs while driving in 95. Second baseman Tony Phillips and outfielder Stanley Javier were excellent role players. Carney Lansford, who had led Santa Clara, California, into the 1969 Little League World Series in Williamsport, Pennsylvania, was all grown up and hit .336. Dave Henderson drove in 80 runs, catcher Terry Steinbach was the class of the league, and Dave Parker knocked in 97 runs. The A's won going away (99–63), then annihilated the out-gunned Toronto Blue Jays in the league championship series, four games to one.

Rickey Henderson's performance against the Blue Jays ranks as one of the most dominant postseason efforts ever: .400 batting average, five RBIs, two home runs, *eight stolen bases*. On to the World Series against...San Francisco! A Bay Bridge Series. Throughout baseball history, the New York Yankees had frequently played against the New York Giants, Brooklyn Dodgers, and in 2000 the Mets. The St. Louis Browns played the St. Louis Cardinals in 1944. The Chicago Cubs took on the White Sox in 1906.

But since baseball moved to the West Coast, the A's had never played the Giants, and the Dodgers had never played the Angels. San Francisco had two legitimate stars. The 1989 National League Most Valuable Player was Kevin Mitchell. Mitchell, who swung at anything when he was a teenage minor leaguer at Kingsport, Tennessee, of the Appalachian League in 1981, had matured, gotten stronger, and learned how to hit. In 1989 he slammed 47 home runs and drove in 125.

His teammate was a good ol' boy from Louisiana who had little love for Mitchell. First baseman Will Clark was in his prime: .333 with 111 RBIs and an unreal .650 average in the playoff victory over Greg Maddux and Chicago.

That was all San Francisco had, however. The A's won the first two in Oakland. Game 3 was to be played at Candlestick Park and I would attend. At 5:04 PM, approximately 11 minutes before the scheduled first pitch, just as Tim McCarver and Al Michaels were making TV introductions, a 7.1 magnitude earthquake centered in Loma Prieta, a north central town about two hours south of San Francisco, rocked the city, the bay, and the baseball world.

A section of the San Francisco Bay Bridge collapsed, killing a driver. The 880/Cypress interchange, part of what traffic reporters call the "maze," collapsed on numerous cars, killing multiple drivers.

I was sitting in the upper deck at Candlestick, and the earthquake at first felt like fans stomping their feet. When people realized what it was, those familiar with earthquakes cheered. Initially it did not seem to threaten the game, although the McCarver-Michaels reaction on TV was alarming.

Then people noticed chunks of the old stadium had cracked. Reports filtered in: the crushed overpass in Oakland, a section of the

That baseball great Joe DiMaggio, a San Francisco native and A's coach in 1968, had his Marina-district home saved by firemen during the 1989 earthquake? In order to prevent a fire, the firemen had to break his window, causing some minor damage to the million-dollar property and some of his belongings. Upon reentering the saved home and seeing some broken glass, the recalcitrant DiMag exclaimed, "f——ing firemen," cursing them out with a stream of expletives for their efforts.

Bay Bridge collapsed (I had been under it on the BART an hour before), fires and sunken homes in the Marina, which is built on landfill. Reports of the single collapsed section of the upper deck of the Bay Bridge made it sound like the entire structure had collapsed in a spectacular bay freefall. Images of downed skyscrapers and other fantastic possibilities at first shocked the folks. The players gathered their families on the field in front of the dugouts. The game was canceled. I engaged in a five-hour odyssey of buses, cable cars, boats, and trains to get out of the city.

When the Series resumed 12 days later, nobody really cared that much about Oakland's continued dominance. They swept San Francisco in Candlestick, which after inspections was said to be structurally sound and is still the home of the 49ers.

"We knew going in that we were the better team," recalled Eckersley, "but after the quake, when we won, it was like, so what, because it no longer really meant anything."

"Big Mac"

Mark "Big Mac" McGwire and pitching star Randy "the Big Unit" Johnson were teammates on some of legendary coach Rod Dedeaux's last teams at the University of Southern California. The Trojans were loaded. Sid Akins pitched for the 1984 U.S. Olympic team. Right-hander Mickey Meister led the Redwood Giants to the national championship, was considered the finest prep hurler in the nation, and was USC's staff ace as a sophomore. Catcher Jack Del Rio, an All-American in football who later played for the Minnesota Vikings before becoming the coach of the Jacksonville Jaguars, was considered the best all-around athlete in the nation.

Stanford had baseball-football star John Elway and future Giant Mike Aldrete. UCLA was led by Shane Mack, but the Trojans' main rival was Arizona State. First, there was Oddibe McDowell, an All-American who later played for the Texas Rangers, but the Sun Devils' prize was an outfielder from Serra High School in San Mateo named Barry Bonds!

The other players would leave the scene, but Bonds, "Big Unit," and "Big Mac," as he was already known at USC, would dominate baseball for 20 years. McGwire came out of Damien High, a Catholic school in Claremont just east of Los Angeles. His father was a dentist, one of his brothers a quarterback with the Seattle Seahawks (Mark's advice to him before his college debut was to "go deep"). McGwire was drafted as a pitcher but took a scholarship to USC instead. After his freshman year, he played for the Fairbanks (Alaska) Goldpanners, a storied summer team in the "land of the midnight sun." After McGwire led the Alaskan League in hitting, Dedeaux nixed plans to use him as a pitcher/third baseman, turning McGwire into a full-time first baseman.

As a sophomore in 1983, McGwire hit 19 home runs, earning All-America honors. In 1984 he was the National Player of the Year, blasting a then–Pac 10–record 32 homers with 80 runs batted in and a .387 batting average. In 1983 USC was edged out of the NCAA playoffs by Bonds's Sun Devils. In 1984 Barry and Arizona State won the Pac 10 South. McGwire and Johnson's Trojans made the Fresno regionals, but despite all their talent, they were ignominiously beaten by Cal State Fullerton and Fresno State.

That summer, McGwire played on what many felt was the best amateur team in U.S. history: the 1984 United States Olympic baseball team. Coached by Dedeaux, the team also featured Will Clark,

Mark McGwire had a short, quick stroke. In 1987 he set a major league record for home runs by a rookie with 49.

Rafael Palmeiro, and Bobby Thigpen (Bonds had to take summer classes to stay NCAA eligible, so he did not play). Just as the loaded Trojans lost in the NCAA playoffs, so too did the United States lose to Japan in the Olympics, which were played at Dodger Stadium.

McGwire was tall and husky but not yet the massive man he would be in the 1990s. He was a nice guy who liked to drink a little beer without going overboard and watch *Cheers*. When his teammates engaged in typical collegiate promiscuity, he avoided trouble. He was a fastidious type who lived at the Regal Trojan Arms, maintaining his room in the orderly fashion of an army recruit in basic training.

McGwire was the first-round draft pick of the A's. During his minor league years, he returned to L.A. in the winter and would socialize with his old friends at USC games until heading off to spring training. In 1986 he came up at season's end. In 1987 he set the big-league record of 49 rookie homers, but his then-wife (a former USC batgirl) gave birth to his son on the last day of the season. McGwire gave up his shot at 50 homers to be at the birth of his son.

McGwire was miffed at being overshadowed by Canseco, a feeling that never bubbled to the surface but was obvious to those close to the team. He was not pleased with Canseco's *Girls Gone Wild* lifestyle. The conservative, Catholic McGwire eschewed a planned autograph-signing session at a San Francisco cigar store when he learned the store sold pornography. During his first three or four years in the major leagues, he remained accessible to his old friends, regularly returning calls and posing for pictures when old pals would bring their kids to the stadium.

But something began to happen in 1991. McGwire divorced his wife and took up with another girl he had known at USC, but the relationship did not flower. He went into a deep depression, batting .201 with 22 home runs on a 1991 A's club that tailed off badly in a year in which Minnesota won the World Series.

In 1992 he rebounded with 42 home runs and never looked back. He was one of baseball's all-time greatest sluggers over the next 10 years, but a retrospective of the early 1990s is revealing. First, McGwire's older brother was a bodybuilder. McGwire had always lifted weights but stopped in 1991 when he went through his second failed romance in a few short years. In 1992 he went back to the weights, claiming the mental edge of strength training was as productive to his performance as the pure physical benefits. In 2005 Canseco claimed that sometime during this period he introduced McGwire to steroids, even injecting him in a bathroom stall. McGwire denied it at first but then went into a seclusion from which he has yet to emerge.

In 1993–1994, McGwire was constantly hurt. Like Canseco, his were abnormal injuries to his feet, arches, back, tendons—all the telltale signs of steroid use. His physique became massive in a short period of time, accentuated by a biker-style goatee. And his personal life changed. He lost touch with old friends, stopped returning calls. His pals became the bodybuilders, guys at the gym. His size, celebrity, and baseball wealth made women available to him. Old USC teammates got shut out.

Craig Stevenson, a Trojan mate and Astros minor leaguer, was his roommate and the best man at his wedding. Craig had to call Mark's agent to get in touch with him. Randy Robertson, a boyhood pal and Claremont American Legion and USC teammate who played in the San Diego organization, received similar treatment. Terry Marks, an SC teammate who has since risen to become a giant of corporate America at Coca-Cola, was shunned by McGwire. When Marks sent items for his old pal to sign for his son, there was no response. Approached in the visitors' locker room at Pac Bell Park, McGwire winced when asked if he still stayed in touch with his teammates from USC.

"That's just not a part of my life anymore," he stated.

Anybody who has ever experienced the camaraderie of team sports knows that this is a very strange attitude. When Dedeaux passed away in 2006, McGwire, living a few miles away in Orange County, made no appearance of any kind. Since his embarrassing performance in front of senatorial steroid investigators in 2005, he has been as reclusive as Greta Garbo.

When all is said and done, McGwire probably will get the Hall vote, although not on the previously slam-dunk first ballot. He will probably go in as a Cardinal, where he put up shocking numbers (70

TOP 10

All-Time Single-Season Home-Run Leaders

1. *Barry Bonds, 73 (2001)
2. ***Mark McGwire, 70 (1998)**
3. *Sammy Sosa, 66 (1998)
4. ***Mark McGwire, 65 (1999)**
5. *Sammy Sosa, 64 (2001)
6. *Sammy Sosa, 63 (1999)
7. **Roger Maris, 61 (1961)**
8. Babe Ruth, 60 (1927)
9. Babe Ruth, 59 (1921)
10. **Jimmie Foxx, 58 † (1932)**
    *Mark McGwire, 58 † (1997)
    Ryan Howard, 58 † (2006)

Additional A's

1. ***Mark McGwire, 52 (1996)**
2. **Jimmie Foxx, 50 (1938)**
3. **Mark McGwire, 49 (1987)**
4. **Jimmie Foxx, 48 (1933)**
5. **Dave Kingman, 48 (1979)**
6. **Reggie Jackson, 47 (1969)**
7. ***Jose Canseco, 46 (1998)**

*Player accused of steriod use

Players shown in bold played for the A's at some point in their careers.

homers in 1998, 65 in 1999). McGwire was most prickly dealing with the media during his 1998 chase of Roger Maris's record. He was just engaging and intelligent enough to get the benefit of the doubt, though. He and Sammy Sosa captured America's hearts when the game needed a lift after the 1994 strike. His loving relationship with his batboy son was beautiful, but when questioned McGwire made inane comments that the media should be at home with their kids instead of watching his chase of history.

To the writers, hardworking folks who were there because they were paid to be there and needed to do it in order to *feed* their kids,

TRIVIA

How many USC baseball players have been named National Player of the Year?

Answers to the trivia questions are on pages 196–198.

it went over like dead weight. McGwire had a deep desire for privacy, which is understandable. His divorce and later break-up with a girlfriend had become public fodder, which is never fun, but he also accepted the money that came with his pursuit of glory. There was no rule saying he had to play baseball instead of going back to school and becoming an anonymous dentist like his father. As Hyman Roth says to Michael Corleone in *The Godfather II,* "This is the life we have chosen."

His 583 lifetime home-run mark is topped by very few. He retired in a heroic manner after the 2001 season, turning down sure millions from St. Louis when he could have mailed it in. He felt he was short-changing his employers and the fans by virtue of his quick decline (in retrospect probably from steroid-caused injuries or because he stopped juicing, a real double-edged sword).

McGwire's record is tainted in several ways. First, his one world championship came amid 1989 tragedy. His home-run records are as worthy of asterisks as Barry Bonds's. The man he thought himself morally better than, Canseco, allegedly led him on the path of steroid addiction. It was McGwire's breaking of Maris's record that, according to the book *Game of Shadows* (2006), motivated Bonds to juice because he was tired of "the white boy" (McGwire) getting all the attention.

A sad tale of fallen heroes, but despite his shortcomings, Big Mac has a good heart and desires to help those less fortunate.

Stew

In Glenn Dickey's 2002 book, *Champions*, Dave Stewart said of the 1990 A's, "We had bad chemistry all year. It all centered on Jose. It was all about Jose."

Canseco missed 31 more games in 1990, again telltale effects of steroid abuse, but if "bad chemistry" and Canseco's injuries slowed this team down, then one must conclude that with a good attitude and no injuries, they would have won 115 regular-season games instead of the 103 they did win. They dominated. McGwire hit 39 homers with 108 RBIs, Canseco 37 with 101 RBIs. Rickey Henderson's .325 average, 28 hits, and 61 RBIs with a league-leading 65 steals from the leadoff spot earned him the MVP award.

Eck was out of his mind: 48 saves and a *0.61 earned-run average.* Bob Welch was 27–6 with a 2.95 ERA, earning him the Cy Young Award. But the staff ace was Stewart (22–11 with a 2.56 ERA and a no-hitter versus Toronto). As Stew went, so went the A's. Good pitching beats good hitting, and this adage was proven true during Oakland's run, both in their favor and to their detriment.

Welch won the Cy Young that Stew never won. In other years, the winner was the heralded Roger Clemens, Frank Viola, Bret Saberhagen, or another teammate, Eckersley. Nobody in 2007 will look back at the careers of Clemens and Stewart and conclude that Stew was better, but in head-to-head matchups between the two—when all was on the line—he most definitely was. In fact, it took years for Clemens to finally win the big games that erased memories of his imploding against Oakland while Stew calmly shut the Red Sox down.

When Stew was on, the A's won the playoffs and the World Series. If he could be out-dueled, as happened versus the Dodgers in

1988, or if he was off, as happened against Cincinnati in 1990, none of his teammates were able to pick up the team enough to rescue it from defeat. He won 20 every year from 1987 to 1990 but never dominated in that manner again. In 1992 he showed a flash of that brilliance, staving off Toronto in an eventual disastrous playoff loss, the last fling of an era. He pitched in the major leagues until 1995, sometimes effectively, becoming one of those guys contenders pick up for the stretch run, but fell short of the Cooperstown status of Eckersley, McGwire, and Henderson.

Stew grew up in Oakland, playing at St. Elizabeth's High School. He came up with Los Angeles, a tremendous prospect. An unfortunate off-field incident shadowed his early career, and

Dave Stewart came out of Oakland's St. Elizabeth's High School but did not live up to his promise until the A's gave him an opportunity. A great competitor, his success in a heated rivalry with Boston's Roger Clemens strengthened his legendary status.

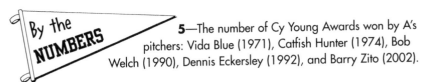

5—The number of Cy Young Awards won by A's pitchers: Vida Blue (1971), Catfish Hunter (1974), Bob Welch (1990), Dennis Eckersley (1992), and Barry Zito (2002).

he seemed to have flamed out until the A's rescued him. Under La Russa he flourished.

"I had been with a couple of organizations that had given up on me," said Stewart. "I hoped the A's would give me a chance to show what I could do, and they did. Dave Duncan sat down with me and talked about baseball, about what it took to win in the major leagues. That was a tremendous help to me, because he really helped me to focus."

Pitching coach Duncan helped him perfect a forkball.

"That made him a three-pitch pitcher, and made all the difference to him," recalled Duncan.

The effectiveness of Stewart's third pitch, and the true nature of big-league excellence, was made very apparent to the Cal-Berkeley team that faced him in an exhibition game at the Oakland Coliseum in 1991. The view from the dugout is more acute than from the stands. The Golden Bears had the best offensive team in school history that year, but their hitters were totally in awe of Stewart's combination of power and forkball.

The first time La Russa told Stewart he was facing Clemens in a big, nationally televised game, Stew replied, "Give me that ball."

"Roger and I had some great duels, and I usually won," recalled Stew in Glenn Dickey's *Champions.* "Roger liked to throw at hitters, but he never did in our games because he knew I'd throw at his hitters. So in a sense, I took away one of his weapons."

TRIVIA

What was Boston pitcher Roger Clemens's record against the A's in championship series play?

Answers to the trivia questions are on pages 196–198.

Shakespeare's Closer

He was the hottest young prospect to break into major league baseball in the mid-1970s. He lived up to the promise in Cleveland and Boston for the better part of five years. He was, like many before him, the archetypal California wild child, with flowing hair and matinee-idol good looks. Like one of those Californians, teammate Bill "Spaceman" Lee, he loved the Boston nightlife, relishing the rock-star status Beantowners accord their baseball heroes. Like many others, it all flamed out too soon, the fault of too much alcohol, not enough sleep, and too little respect for the game.

He was a symbol of wasted youth and misspent talent. His brother was convicted of murder, and the young hero seemed destined to be the baseball player who Bruce Springsteen meets heading into a roadside bar in "Glory Days"—the guy who could "throw that speedball by ya"—or worse.

Then, in 1987, Walt Jocketty traded Dave Wilder, an outfielder from Berkeley High and Cal State Fullerton, along with two minor league pitchers to the Chicago Cubs for Dennis Eckersley. Just as when he picked up Oakland's Dave Stewart, Jocketty probably felt that a return to his hometown might revive Eckersley's career—maybe provide a year or so of occasional highlights before retirement.

Eckersley, a 6'2", 195-pound, Oakland-born right-hander from Washington High School in Fremont, found more than a second chance with the A's. It was more than redemption. It was total rebirth and the opportunity to achieve everything that had been expected of him 12 years earlier—and then much, much more.

Eck went well above and beyond being just a good pitcher with a fine big-league career. He became a Hall of Famer and very possibly

DID YOU KNOW . . . That the A's of the 1988 through 1992 championship period had six players from Bay Area high schools on their team? They include Rickey Henderson (Oakland Tech), Carney Lansford (Santa Clara Wilcox), Willie McGee (Oakland Castlemont), Lance Blankenship (Concord Ygnacio Valley), Dave Stewart (Oakland St. Elizabeth's), and Dennis Eckersley (Fremont Washington).

the finest relief pitcher of all time. His second chance strengthened him, and he needed it.

In 1988 and 1992 he gave up game-winning home runs at the worst possible time in postseason games, to Kirk Gibson of Los Angeles in 1988 and Roberto Alomar of Toronto in 1992. He rebounded from these disasters, both of which would have set him back mentally for weeks, months, in his previous incarnation.

"It knocked me down for a couple of weeks," Eckersley said of the 1988 home-run pitch to Gibson. "Then I had time to reflect on all the good things that happened to me that year. I couldn't let that one thing spoil all of that. I wouldn't be much of a person if I did."

In 1989 Eck came back to post 55 strikeouts with an unbelievable three walks in 57⅔ innings, 33 saves, and a 1.56 earned-run average; then total dominance in the playoffs (three saves) and World Series (closing out the clincher at Candlestick).

"I wanted to show that the year wasn't a fluke," he said. "I wanted to show the skeptics and I wanted to prove it to myself."

The Shakespearean nature of Eck's career came in the way success always seemed to come to Eck—tempered by offsetting failure. In 1990 he was off the charts with a 0.61 ERA, 48 saves, and the mind-boggling 73 strikeouts versus four bases on balls in 73⅓ innings. In 1992 he earned the Cy Young *and* MVP awards with a 7–1 record, a 1.91 ERA, 51 saves, 93 strikeouts, and 11 walks in 80 innings. Toronto was again Oakland's championship series opponent. They were a widely disparaged "Canadian import," known mostly for post-season failure, derided as the "Blow Jays." Eck seemed to be in control as usual, until he suffered another Gibson moment worthy of *Hamlet* or *Macbeth*.

Seemingly out of nowhere, Robbie Alomar hammered an Eckersley pitch into the right-field seats at the Coliseum to break

Oakland's hearts. Stewart clutched up the next day, winning to send the series back to Toronto, but the air had been taken out of Oakland's tires. The Jays won, then beat Atlanta in the World Series. The "Blow Jays" moniker was gone, only to be hung unceremoniously on Eck's and his team's neck.

There was much blame to go around: La Russa was too tight-fisted; Canseco could have made the difference, but he was traded at

No relief pitcher has ever been more dominant than Hall of Famer Dennis Eckersley was from 1988 to 1992. Photo courtesy of AP/Wide World Photos.

midseason because he was not a team player; McGwire was impressive with his newfound strength, which was window dressing in a losing display.

But it was Eck who had given up shot-heard-'round-the-world-style home runs twice in four years. It all fit into the pattern of his life. A sidewinding right-hander who pointed at hitters after striking them out, an act

TRIVIA

Dennis Eckersley prepped at Washington High School in Fremont, about a half-hour drive south of the Coliseum. What famous football coach got his start coaching at Washington?

Answers to the trivia questions are on pages 196–198.

that engendered some animosity, alleging he was "showing up" beaten foes. Eck knew, as Richard Nixon once said, "that one can never know what it is like to be on the highest mountain until he has been in the lowest valley."

Eck came out of the Bay Area in the "lost generation" of the 1970s. It was a time and place of drugs, alcohol, and ennui. He liked to party. His looks made him the star of the "neon league," which describes the watering holes that players frequent from coast to coast. His attempts to settle down were frustrated by his alcohol addiction. He was finally shamed into quitting by a home video showing him incapacitated in the presence of his children at a Christmas party. When the A's gave him another chance, he rose like Lazarus to find his best self, on and off the field. He had won 20 in Boston and thrown a no-hitter for Cleveland, but the bullpen was the best forum for his immense talents.

He was the best of the best from 1988 to 1992, but ultimate victory (the 1989 championship) was tempered, as it was for that whole star-crossed team, by disaster. But in a way that motivated him. Eck feared failure, which to his mind was always lurking just around the corner. As it stands, it was.

"Eckersley was driven by his fear of failure," A's announcer Bill King said. "He was the opposite of Ken Stabler, who never feared a thing, but Eck scared himself into succeeding as if the alternative was too horrible to contemplate."

The Clubhouse Lawyer

Tony La Russa came from the sun-kissed fields of Tampa, Florida, one of the hotbeds of baseball talent in America. His boyhood pal was Lou Piniella, who had success with the Royals and Yankees and more of the same as a manager.

La Russa was considered the better prospect, a bonus baby who came up with Finley's A's in the 1960s. He never panned out. While his friend was winning world championships in New York, La Russa toiled in obscurity, struggling to break out of a career in the minor leagues. A very smart fellow, La Russa made provisions for his life, going to school in the off-season and eventually obtaining a law degree.

But he was drawn back to baseball. His sharp mind and the fact that he paid attention to the game all those years made him a managerial prospect. He led the White Sox to the 1983 American League West title before losing to Baltimore in the playoffs. Baseball fickleness set in, and when his success did not continue, neither did he as Chicago's manager.

The A's, a team being built from the ground up throughout the 1980s by Walt Jocketty and Sandy Alderson, liked his ephemeral style. The Billy Martin experience had soured them on "old school" baseball people. Alderson in particular was of a new breed. He did not play baseball and had little organized experience with the game. A former marine officer, once an actual poster boy for the Corps, he was also an Ivy League lawyer. He married into the Haas family and was put to work on legal and contractual matters. His grasp of union rules, contractual details, and the Players' Agreement, negotiated periodically with the owners (and the cause of strikes in 1972, 1981, and 1994), made him indispensable. Over time, his knowledge of the game grew to that of an expert's. He became the general manager and architect of Oakland's success.

He and La Russa were a perfect fit, and La Russa was perfect for the Bay Area. His politics seemed to lean a bit to the left, although details never were revealed. But he was a big environmentalist, a "bleeding heart" whose pet charity was animal protection.

Despite his cerebral approach, La Russa's blood could boil. Writers were always hard-pressed to get him to smile. A seething temper often seemed to simmer below the surface, much like it did

Manager Tony La Russa (right) ushered in the era of computers as a baseball tool, and his intellectual approach has led to a new breed of managers and general managers.

That A's manager Tony La Russa was considered one of the finest prospects in baseball when he graduated from high school in Tampa, Florida, in 1962? He was only 18 years old when he made his major league debut with the Kansas City A's in 1963. After spending five additional years in the minors, he returned to the bigs with Oakland in 1968, but he could never break into the lineup, eventually retiring. His less-heralded Tampa friend, Lou Piniella, became the star.

with Piniella. The unspoken feeling among players and media was that one did not want to get on his bad side, that he was patient but, pushed to a certain point, could explode—and it would not be pretty.

The La Russa–Alderson style changed baseball. It certainly became the "A's way," still firmly held together by Billy Beane. La Russa loved computers. He and pitching coach Dave Duncan fed endless streams of information into them, determining every possible permutation and advantage based on right-left matchups, tendencies of hitters and pitchers in varied situations, statistics in day games versus night games, and the like. It was the exact opposite of Joe Schultz, manager of the 1969 Seattle Pilots. Pitcher Jim Bouton wrote in *Ball Four* that he presented Schultz with charts and graphs demonstrating when he should most effectively be used, whereupon Schultz replied, "I don't need to look at that stuff. I watch the games."

La Russa's detractors over the years, in Oakland and St. Louis, have said he overthinks, and they may have a point, but he represented the thinking that went into a game changed by economics. For years, the length of a baseball season tended to deaden the importance of any single game. "We'll get 'em tomorrow" was the refrain. But when big money hit in the 1970s and '80s, followed by ESPN, big TV contracts, and a plethora of new stadiums, the need to draw large audiences to the games and to the tube increased the importance of regular-season contests. In New York, owner George Steinbrenner accepted nothing less than total commitment to each victory.

La Russa was not the sort to let wins and losses seep out of memory without lessons learned. He did not "pound Budweiser" after games, as

Schultz did, but rather reviewed film, crunched numbers, and gave each of the 162 games the kind of preparation a football coach gives to his once-a-week schedule.

His background and approach, the Ivy League education of Alderson, then other general managers, notably

TRIVIA

Aside from La Russa and Piniella, who are some other baseball greats from Tampa, Florida?

Answers to the trivia questions are on pages 196–198.

Red Sox wunderkind Theo Epstein, gave rise to the Moneyball era of the 2000s. A split occurred in baseball between scouts and organization men who strictly value baseball experience over nontraditional baseball people, "fantasy leaguers" whose use of new technologies created a paradigm shift in scouting, development, and strategy. The success of Beane, Epstein, and a number of young GMs in recent years seems to indicate that the new breed is winning over the traditionalists, but the argument has the potential to be a longstanding one with little real resolution.

In La Russa's case, his Oakland success is marred by the four-game World Series loss to Cincinnati, which stands out as the greatest sore spot on his record. Facing La Russa's old pal, Cincinnati manager Lou Piniella, the A's came in loaded for bear. La Russa's take on the Series, as described in Glenn Dickey's *Champions,* follows:

> That season, we had won 103 games, but I thought we won some of those games on reputation. There were some slippages. When we got to our third postseason, we had lost our edge. It wasn't new anymore, and we were strutting around. Cincinnati just beat us to the punch in every way. To this day, I think of the '88 Series as a lost opportunity, but '90 is the one that bothers me the most. I don't think you ever take it lightly when you get to the World Series. But I blame myself. When we had a meeting before the Series, I could tell they weren't listening. I probably should have yelled and screamed, but I didn't. When we went out there, we were totally flat.

A King Walked among Us

The man was an artist. The da Vinci, Michelangelo, or Frank Lloyd Wright of broadcasting.

Bill King was the longtime announcer for the Oakland A's, and before that he was the voice of the Raiders, Warriors, Giants, and California Golden Bears. He had one of the most recognizable deliveries in sports. The goateed Sausalito resident was a highly recognizable Bay Area figure who was once stopped and asked if he was the devil.

The man was a talkative angel.

"I always liked to talk," said the Bloomington, Illinois, native during a 2001 Coliseum interview. He got his start in broadcasting with the Armed Forces Radio Network while stationed in the Mariana Islands after World War II.

"It was great duty. I guess you could say I was the 'Robin Williams of Guam,'" said King, referring to Williams's role as Adrian Cronauer in *Good Morning, Vietnam*.

Like so many veterans, King migrated to California and was the right man in the right spot when the Giants brought major league baseball to San Francisco.

"I worked with Russ Hodges and Lon Simmons on Giants games on KSFO," recalled King.

"Football by far is the hardest sport to do," he said. "Basketball is the easiest. In baseball, you have to be careful when you open your mouth not to show how stupid you are."

King announced California football as well as the 1960 Bears' national championship basketball team, coached by the legendary Pete Newell.

King achieved his most lasting fame announcing the most dramatic moments of the most exciting team in pro football history, the Al Davis Oakland Raiders of the 1960s, '70s, and '80s. He followed the team to Los Angeles from 1982 to 1994 but left in a dispute with Davis when the team returned to Oakland in 1995.

"Davis is a fascinating man," King said of the mysterious Raiders owner. "He coached and was commissioner of the AFL."

Bill King died in 2005, after spending his life announcing for the A's, Warriors, Oakland and L.A. Raiders, Giants, and Cal football and basketball. For those who heard him over the years, he is regarded as possibly the finest all-around sports announcer who ever lived. This photo shows his favorite chair from the A's broadcast booth on the night of his 2006 memorial service. Photo courtesy of AP/Wide World Photos.

Was Davis the "genius" behind the wide-open passing game of the old American Football League?

"Sid Gillman was the real force of the new offensive philosophy of the AFL," exclaimed King, referring to the former San Diego Chargers coach, "but Al absorbed those philosophies. Interestingly, though, nobody won with over 40 passes in those days."

In 1970 backup quarterback George Blanda passed and kicked the team to a series of miraculous wins. King's legend was made when he said, "George Blanda is king of the world" after he kicked a long field goal to beat Cleveland. His "Wells to the right, Biletnikoff slot left" was a trademark, too, but two phrases define King's football broadcasts.

One stems from the Raiders' 1974 AFC playoff win over Miami, when he stated, "Raiders: two yards from the promised land" just before Clarence Davis's touchdown grab gave them victory.

The other is "Holy Toledo," which King used mostly to describe touchdowns but also homers and great defensive plays. "It's better than saying 'holy s——,'" was King's explanation.

"Ken Stabler was a delight," King said. "He's the only athlete I've ever known who had no fear of failure. He's the converse of Dennis Eckersley, who like most athletes drove himself through fear of failure.

"The Raiders' party scene was overhyped, but I will say that their rowdiness at the El Rancho Tropicana in Santa Rosa lived up to the legend. John Madden was fairly true to the image of him, but he was totally absorbed in his job. Now, he truly loves what he does, because he's glad not to have to have the tunnel vision required of a head coach."

DID YOU KNOW ... That Bill King had curious likes and dislikes? One of his dislikes was the state of Texas. In later years, he arranged vacation time during the season based on when the A's visited Arlington in the summer. Also, despite his reputation as an intellectual sort, King often did games in Speedo shorts. He often just wore sandals, giving the appearance of an aging hippie. His cohorts constantly teased him for his voracious appetite, too.

King was a literate man who made references to the likes of Aristotle and Fitzgerald, among others, but he "cannot explain what comes out of my mouth."

King saw all the great ones.

"Rick Barry is intelligent and has a huge ego," King said, "but I'm always sorry when I hear him say some of the disparaging things that get him in trouble."

King supported Ray Guy as a Football Hall of Famer but was not sure of Stabler's qualifications. One thing is for sure: King has Hall of Fame credentials in at least two sports.

His football days are a distant memory to Bay Area fans, since his last 12 years with the Raiders were in Los Angeles (although all those games were broadcast in the Bay Area). King's basketball announcing is even more remote. To younger fans, he will be remembered as a baseball man, consistently handling microphone chores for Oakland from the early 1980s through the 2005 season. Sadly, he passed away during relatively minor surgery in October 2005. A's announcers Ray Fosse and Ken Korach revered King.

TRIVIA

Which Giants executive was once an A's announcer?

Answers to the trivia questions are on pages 196–198.

Among old-time fans, King was like a part of the family. His great moments of the 1960s and 1970s often occurred in radio-only games. Real sports aficionados all have "King stories." One of the most cogent arguments among them is whether King was best in football, basketball, or baseball.

There is no answer. He simply epitomized excellence and professionalism, with a wonderful touch of color, humor, and ironic twist. Had he announced tiddlywinks, he would have developed a fan base.

Hey, We All Know about Jason Giambi

Oh, scouting. It is not an exact science. Ask the guys who passed up on Mike Piazza when the kid was lifting weights to develop a chiseled body, demonstrating the kind of work ethic that legends are made of, while attending high school in Pennsylvania. Looking back, it would seem obvious that, although Mike might not have been first-round material, this guy deserved a shot.

It was only because he is Tommy Lasorda's godson that the Dodgers did his father, Vince, a favor by selecting him in the 62nd round out of Miami Dade Junior College.

Remember Wes Parker? Slick-fielding All-Star first sacker, a Dodgers favorite in the 1960s? If you were checking this glovemeister out when he was growing up in the rich Brentwood enclave of L.A., you would surely figure he would help any major league club, right? Not so.

Parker was a rich kid who had to beg his next-door neighbor, a Kansas City A's scout, to sign him. The scout told him to go to college; he could afford tuition at USC or an Ivy League school. Parker insisted, so, according to Parker, the scout signed him as a free agent. The next thing they knew, Wes was winning Gold Gloves and helping the team to the 1965 world championship.

Then, of course, you have your Todd Van Poppels and David Clydes. The list of great preps who never panned out after signing for the big dough is just too long and depressing to get into here. Besides, the point is made. Scouting is not an exact science!

Which brings us to Jason Giambi. Big guy, impressive, a great swing, natural athlete. Somehow 42 rounds went by before the Milwaukee Brewers saw fit to select Giambi after his senior year at

South Hills High School in baseball-crazy West Covina, California. Looking at this guy mash it makes it hard to believe nobody saw the potential—that is, until the BALCO investigation revealed more than we may have wanted to know.

Giambi spurned a low Brewers offer and instead lit it up for Coach Dave Snow at powerhouse Cal State Long Beach. "Take that," he seemed to be saying of his draft snub. He was a freshman All-American and 1992 Olympian. So Snow saw what others missed, right?

Wrong.

The 49ers coach, considered one of the best baseball men in the country, tried to turn Giambi into a full-time pitcher, but the kid talked his way into playing a full-time position. That is another aspect of his makeup that somehow has been overlooked: his personality. His will to win, to succeed, to show how good he is—this guy is a competitor.

With all due respect to the baseball intelligentsia who did not see greatness in the high school versions of Jose Canseco, Mark McGwire, Giambi, and others like them, one must take into account

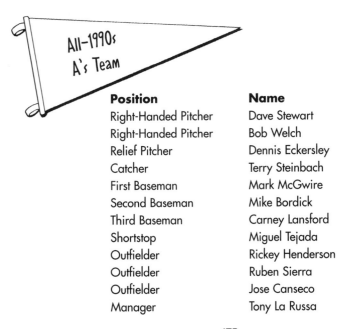

All-1990s
A's Team

Position	Name
Right-Handed Pitcher	Dave Stewart
Right-Handed Pitcher	Bob Welch
Relief Pitcher	Dennis Eckersley
Catcher	Terry Steinbach
First Baseman	Mark McGwire
Second Baseman	Mike Bordick
Third Baseman	Carney Lansford
Shortstop	Miguel Tejada
Outfielder	Rickey Henderson
Outfielder	Ruben Sierra
Outfielder	Jose Canseco
Manager	Tony La Russa

what weight training and, uh, supplements have done to make some players stronger and better.

Giambi is a hard-charger. He likes to party, the chicks dig him, and the dude lived large in Oakland, on the road, and then in the Big Apple. He and his brother, Jeremy, were often seen tooling around San Francisco with Raiders place-kicker Sebastian Janikowski (the guy who thought slipping roofies into girls' drinks was an appropriate way of introducing himself), heading to the latest hot nightclub. However, Jason worked hard, too. He put in the time, and it paid off. Giambi was the starting first baseman for the American League All-Star team in 2000 before winning the MVP award, hitting .333 with 137 RBIs, and achieving a .647 slugging percentage, a .476 on-base percentage, and 137 walks. He was the biggest reason Oakland won their division. He should have beaten out Ichiro Suzuki to repeat as MVP in 2001, an award his good friend (former teammate and fellow East San Gabriel Valley product) Mark McGwire never garnered.

In 2001 Giambi batted .342 with 38 home runs, 120 runs batted in, and 129 walks in his send-off

Jason Giambi came into his own after Mark McGwire left in 1997 and earned the 2000 Most Valuable Player award.

season. Billy Beane could not afford him, and the bright lights of New York were too attractive to a limelight guy like Giambi.

In Oakland, the 6'3", 235-pound Giambi played alongside brother

TRIVIA

How many MVPs have the A's had?

Answers to the trivia questions are on pages 196–198.

Jeremy, a Cal State Fullerton product, who might have matched numbers with Jason had he known BALCO's Victor Conte a little better. Eventually, Jeremy's failure to slide against New York on the famed Derek Jeter backhand toss of the 2001 playoffs, combined with his enthusiasm for wine, women, and song, made him persona non grata in Oaktown.

Jason, however, was *the man* in Oakland, where he shared an East Bay apartment with his bro before getting hitched. The two lived in Las Vegas in the off-season. SoCal Giambi always had the casual, inside-knowledge insouciance of a New Yorker and has been known to intimate that some members of his Italian clan are, well, connected. Whether they are or not, no one is saying, but Jason just loved that kind of thing. He is flashy, drives a Lamborghini, and in 2002 became one of the highest-paid athletes in the world. Still, he is not money-hungry, as evidenced by the fact that he signed for less than market value ($10 million for three years) to stay with the potential-dynasty A's after the 1998 season.

Giambi actually follows in the tradition of another former Oakland Athletic, Jose Canseco, in that he commands a lot of attention, not always for his on-field activities, but seems to be handling everything pretty well. Party on, man.

Hudson and the A's Had the Time of Their Lives

Major league pitchers are supposed to be monsters. Six feet, six inches tall, 225 pounds of twisted steel and sex appeal. A three-day growth outlining a goatee worthy of any Hell's Angel. Wrestlers' legs and a big backside.

Tim Hudson had the goatee. Kind of.

Other than that, the similarity of Hudson and the prototypical big-league stud ended there. Two of his pitching mates on the Oakland A's of the early 2000s, southpaws Barry Zito and Mark Mulder, had their pictures in *Webster's* next to the words *typical big-league hurler*. Not so the height-challenged Hudson. The A's media guide listed him as 6'1", which stretched credulity. He did not sniff 6' unless he wore platforms.

Huddie and his pals liked to have fun, too.

"Jason decides where we'll go," Oakland's ace right-hander said of Scottsdale nightlife during spring training in 2001. "We just follow."

Hudson, of course, was talking about Jason Giambi, then-reigning American League MVP, self-described "connected" Italian American ("My uncle lives in Las Vegas, you know"), all-around bon vivante and man about town.

Observers of the baseball scene have noted in recent years that these new young professionals like to read *The Wall Street Journal* and talk business on cell phones with their agents. Where is the fun in baseball? The camaraderie and friendship?

Oakland was alive and well when Giambi was there. The A's modeled themselves after Jason, a guy who trained as hard as his good friend and ex-teammate Mark McGwire. Like George Brett in a previous generation, he liked to have fun but was always ready to play ball when the bell rang.

So were his teammates. They were young, good-looking guys, though, and liked to enjoy life.

"We go to Maloney's, maybe Sanctuary," said Hudson of the hopping Phoenix/Scottsdale nightlife.

"In Oakland," Hudson continued, "we stay more low-key. Guys usually live in the Pleasanton, San Ramon, area, and we'll occasionally

Tim Hudson came off the campus of Auburn University to help form the ace pitching staff that propelled Oakland's success in the new millennium. Photo courtesy of AP/Wide World Photos.

Hudson was the first A's ace. When opponents lined up their rotations before facing Oakland, it was with Hudson in mind. Guys were asked to play hurt when Hudson was scheduled, because opponents would need everything they had. Managers would bunt in the first inning, play little ball.

"I mean, I can handle it," acknowledged Hudson. "I don't back down from the challenge, I love it. It's what makes you what you are."

Case study number one came early in the 2001 season, when the New York Yankees came to town. They had Roger Clemens ready for Hudson. In a game that reminded longtime A's aficionados of classic 1970s duels between Catfish Hunter and Jim Palmer, neither figured in the decision, an extra-inning 3–2 Oakland win.

"Facing Clemens was definitely exciting," said Hudson. "Going up against Pedro Martinez, Randy Johnson—with the stadium packed. It's just fun to be on the same field with future Hall of Famers. From the short time I've been here, a year and a half, I think I've earned respect."

Hudson drifted ever so slightly, and you could see him mentally pinch himself. At 5'10", 160 pounds, he overcame the size factor.

"I was 5'10", 145 in high school," he said. "That's one reason I got overlooked. My high school coach, Russ Martin, helped me, as did my summer coach, a guy named Flint Sharpe, who coached a team called the Dixie Boys."

As you might guess, Hudson is from the South. As in Alabama.

TRIVIA

Tim Hudson (Auburn, SEC), Mark Mulder (Michigan State, Big Ten), and Barry Zito (USC, Pac 10) often argued the merits of their colleges and conferences. Which of those conferences has produced the most Cy Young Award winners?

Answers to the trivia questions are on pages 196–198.

"I didn't pitch until my junior year in high school," he said. "Sharpe taught me the breaker. I just got better and established myself in J.C."

Hudson then transferred to Auburn.

"That was a great opportunity," he said. "Top to bottom, the Southeastern Conference is the best baseball league in the nation. Every once in a while I'll get in a discussion with Zito about the merits of the SEC versus the Pac 10 [Zito is a former

IF ONLY . . . The designated hitter had not been instituted in 1973, the A's may well have had the best collection of good-hitting pitchers baseball has ever known. Catfish Hunter was an excellent hitter. Ken Holtzman had key hits in World Series play. Mark Mulder and Tim Hudson were both great college hitters, denied the chance to swing in Oakland.

USC Trojan]. We faced Stanford and lost in the 1997 College World Series.

"I played for Hal Baird, who was the pitching coach and head coach, and Steve Renfro, who took over as the head coach. Auburn was my first taste of first-class baseball, a terrific program with great facilities like in the big leagues. Coach Renfro and Coach Baird gave me a chance, and I'm still close with them."

He also learned from the great sociological experiment that is professional ball.

"Coming from Alabama," he remarked, "I'd not met many Latinos, but in the minors half the team was speaking Spanish. Luis Vizcaino spoke no English, but my buddy Chad Harville and I would talk, and it was like, 'Luis is a cool guy. I sure wish I could talk to him.' Sometimes I'd have a catcher who couldn't speak English, so we'd communicate through signs."

Hudson was the leader of a young staff.

"I don't know all there is about pitching, but I think I can help, and we tend to look at each other pitch and give advice," he said. "Zito's good taking advice."

Hudson, the country boy from Alabama, could not help ribbing SoCal lefty Zito.

"I know how to get into Zito's head faster than anybody," he said. "He worries about how others perceive him. I like Barry a lot. He never tries to be something he's not. But when he had that blue hair, I mean, I had to get in some ribbing."

Hudson was not the first short-statured pitcher to come from south of the Mason-Dixon Line. Remember "Louisiana Lightning," Ron Guidry?

"Sure," said Hudson. "You can't measure what's in a guy's heart, what his desire is, does he know how to pitch?"

Mulder Stepped Up

Mark Mulder was approached after pitching six innings, allowing four runs with four strikeouts, seven hits, and three walks, in Oakland's victory over San Francisco in a 2001 spring training game at Scottsdale Stadium. He was phenomenal in the first couple of innings, yakking the Giants with a big, slow curveball that had San Francisco hitters standing in the box with the bat in their hands. His two strike-outs in the second inning consisted entirely of called third strikes.

So what did the 6'6" southpaw want to talk about after his impressive effort?

"Michigan State's real good," he said of the Spartans basketball team that was defending their national championship at the Final Four that weekend. "They don't have a Mateen Cleaves, but they're experienced and it's great to see."

You guessed right. Mulder is a Michigan State alum.

"It's great to see," he said. "We never dominated Michigan when I was there, but now it's really looking good."

Mulder was in East Lansing in 1997 and 1998, when he was an All-American pitcher for the Spartans.

"I think the Big Ten's a tougher basketball conference," he said, "but it's not as good as Western and Southern leagues in baseball. It's just too cold. We didn't even get out and play games until our first trip West."

Spring is, naturally, a time for optimism, but the optimism for Mulder or his team back in 2001 was not false. That season, the 6'6", 200-pound left-hander from South Holland, Illinois—a first-round pick by the A's in 1998—won a league-leading 21 games. He followed

That of the 11 A's MVPs, eight signed out of high school? Lefty Grove (1931) and Jimmie Foxx (1932 and 1933) were both from Maryland. Bobby Shantz (1952) was from Maryland. Vida Blue (1971) was from Louisiana. Jose Canseco (1988) came from Miami. Rickey Henderson (1990) was from Oakland, Dennis Eckersley (1992) from Fremont. Miguel Tejada (2002) hails from the Dominican Republic. Jason Giambi (2000) grew up in West Covina and went to Cal State Long Beach. Reggie Jackson (1973) grew up in Baltimore and Pennsylvania before going to Arizona State.

that up with 19 in 2002 and 15 in a season (2003) in which he spent time on the disabled list. His last year in Oakland was 2004, when he won 17.

Mulder was also a good hitter, having swung the bat while playing first base during his nonpitching days at Michigan State. On the hill, he was always a picture of relaxation and self-control.

"There's always been something about Mark that's really hard to describe," said Eric Chavez in Mychael Urban's book *Aces*. "Of all the guys I've played with, he's the one guy that you can honestly say you don't know if he's throwing a no-hitter or getting lit up. It's almost like he doesn't even care sometimes, even though I know that's not true. Obviously, he cares. But if you didn't know him and you were out there, you'd probably think he didn't. I think it's just that he kind of knows how good he is, and he knows that if he does things the right way, there's no need to get excited about anything out there. Just go out there, do your thing, and come back."

"From the moment he came to the big leagues, he felt like he belonged," said pitching coach Curt Young, who knew Mulder since he came up through the minor leagues. "And I think he's kept that same belief from day one. It's just that total belief in himself."

Young said that a "diagram of the perfect pitcher" would result in somebody like the statuesque Mulder, whom he compared to Steve Carlton in that regard.

"The perfect pitcher?" Mulder pondered the question. "I don't know about that. If I was the perfect pitcher, I wouldn't have sucked so bad when I was a rookie."

In that 2000 season, Mulder won nine games. Writers covering the team thought he was difficult to deal with, but with success came maturity and a more pleasant personality.

"Why would I care about what somebody who doesn't know me thinks?" Mulder asked in Urban's *Aces* (2005). "And if someone wants to judge me based on whether I stop and say hi to every single person on the way to my locker, whatever."

Southpaw Mark Mulder had it all.

Mulder loved the perks of base-ball stardom—money, leisure time, and the chance to pursue his other passion: golf. He and Tim Hudson hauled their clubs from city to city. But over time, he found celebrity to be a "drill."

TRIVIA

Which conference—SEC, Big Ten, or Pac 10— has produced the most MVPs?

Answers to the trivia questions are on pages 196–198.

Mulder was off to a fast start in 2004. He seemed to have a shot at the Cy Young Award, but inexplicably he slumped in the second half of the season. There was no obvious explanation, such as fatigue or injury. It was also nothing new for pitchers, a fragile lot.

In 1970 Tom Seaver, fresh off the glory of leading the Amazin' Mets to the world championship, was on top of the world. Early in the season, he tied the all-time single-game record for strikeouts with 19, facing San Diego. In that game, he set the mark for most consecutive K's by setting the final 10 Padres down on strikes. He started the All-Star Game and by early August posted 17 wins. He had stated prior to the season that his goal was to win 30 games. He seemed well on his way.

Then Seaver took a 2–1 lead into the bottom of the ninth on a hot, muggy night in Atlanta. With two outs and the bases loaded, he struck out the last Brave to win the game—except that he crossed up catcher Jerry Grote by throwing a fastball instead of the slider Grote signaled. It got by Grote, allowing the tying run to score. Seaver was so stunned he stood on the mound, failing to cover home. The runner from *second* scored the winning run, 3–2.

Seaver went from a five-day to a four-day rotation in order to get more starts down the stretch. He hit a mental roadblock, only winning one more game all season, costing New York the East Division in a close chase.

Mulder traveled the same perilous journey in 2004. He admitted to thinking too much on the mound and approached Zito, consid-ered a Zen master of sorts, for help. He became the client of Harvey Dorfman, a sports psychologist.

"It was basically him wanting to tell me what I'm out there think-ing and what I'm out there doing, and what's going on," said Mulder.

"Basically, it was his telling me, 'Look, this isn't what you think it is. You're making it more than it really is in your head.'"

It did not work. Like Seaver 34 years earlier, Mulder tanked and it cost his team a postseason berth. On December 18, 2004, Mark was traded to the St. Louis Cardinals for Danny Haren, Kiko Calero, and Daric Barton. Whether Beane saw something in Mulder, some indication that he indeed had "lost it," was not revealed, although rumors flew that Beane was "right" when Mulder got off to a slow start with the Cardinals. Ultimately, he had a good, but not outstanding, season in St. Louis. Haren had an excellent first year with the A's.

Mulder's trade was a sad day for Oakland fans.

Zito

Barry Zito reminds people of Bill Bordley. "Who?" you might ask. Well, to those who saw him, Bordley was the best college pitcher ever. Some people thought he was as good as Sandy Koufax. There are scouts and Pacific 10 umpires who say he was the best pitcher in the world, not just in college, back when he was leading USC to the 1978 national championship.

Zito has the size, the big kick, the hesitation at the top of his motion, and the classic Koufax-style overhand delivery. He brings it at 90 miles per hour, with hop and movement. His curveball crackles.

"He's the real deal," said former USC coach Mike Gillespie, who coached Zito when the tall lefty was the top pitcher in the nation in 1999. Barry became a rich young man when the Oakland A's made him their first pick in the draft. It all happened pretty fast.

Zito grew up in the San Diego area, rooting for the Padres. At University High School, he had a "decent" senior year, threw a fastball that topped out around 83 miles per hour, and was drafted by Seattle in the 59th round in 1996. He was helped with his mechanics by a coach named Craig Weisman, and six months after graduation he was throwing 10 miles per hour harder.

Barry took his 3.1 grade point average to UC–Santa Barbara and Coach Bob Bronsema, which seemed like a pretty good choice at the time. Cal State Northridge and Wake Forest liked him, too, but the SCs, Fullertons, and Miamis of the world had bigger fish to fry.

"SC seemed out of my reach," recalled Barry. "I got full financial aid to Santa Barbara, plus some scholarship help."

It happens to some kids. Tom Seaver went into the marines and came out a ball of muscle. The scout who signed Nolan Ryan claims he threw only 85 miles per hour in high school. How can you explain it? Yes, Barry lifted weights and worked hard, but that can't fully account for his late development. At Santa Barbara he was a freshman All-American, striking out 125 in 85 innings. He was up to 6'3", 195 pounds. The scouts took note of his improved mechanics.

He started working with a San Fernando Valley trainer, Alan Jagger, and figured that he had entered a window of opportunity in which he would be eligible for some big bonus money.

"Santa Barbara just wasn't a high-profile program," he said.

For this reason, he transferred to L.A. Pierce College, although he said his departure from Santa Barbara was "ugly." Zito showcased his wares for the 1998 draft and was 9–2 with a 2.60 ERA and 135 strikeouts in 103 innings.

"The competition just wasn't that good in J.C.," said Barry.

In the end, Barry Zito proved to be the most successful of the A's aces.

After losing to Harbor in the state playoffs, Zito found himself drafted in the third round by Texas. He was intent on signing, but he is a savvy guy who knew his market value. The Rangers came in at $350,000, but Barry held out for more, finally took off for the Cape Cod League, and left his dad in charge of the negotiations. The old man had a hard-nosed reputation, no doubt based on his money demands. Zito made the Cape All-Star team but decided not to sign.

The result was a windfall for Mike Gillespie, who needed a new infusion of talent to replace all the studs who had won him the 1998 national championship. Zito picked SC over Clemson, but he had to go to Grossmont College to get an associate in arts degree first. He enrolled at Southern Cal in January 1999 and immediately assumed the role of ace.

Gillespie loved him, and he loved Gillespie.

"I also experienced Rod Dedeaux," Zito said, recalling the time he met the legendary former coach. Zito was a consensus All-American in 1999, pitching the Trojans past Pepperdine in the West Regional before the team lost a heartbreaking 1–0 decision to Stanford's Jason Young, when a fly ball was lost in the dusk at Sunken Diamond, with the College World Series on the line. For fans that were unaware of Barry's rocky but flashy road, he seemed to be a surprise. Scouts, coaches, Gillespie—they got what they expected.

"The USC-Stanford rivalry is always a battle," Zito said of what is probably the best confrontation in the nation. "They'd come here, win two of three. We'd go there, take two of three."

The disappointment of not pitching Troy to a repeat national title quickly wore off when Billy Beane, the A's boy genius GM and architect of baseball's best story in 1999, made Barry their number one pick. One point six million dollars later, Zito was lighting up the California League, where he was 3–0 with a 2.45 ERA and 62 strikeouts in 40 innings of work at Visalia. In mid-August he found himself in Midland (Double A Texas League), and although he did not schmooze with George W., he did pitch four impressive games.

"It's a tiny town," Zito said of the place where the president grew up. "High school football is huge there."

He was a strikeout pitcher all the way and learned to trust his bullpen—or so he said—but after regularly facing 130-pitch limits, when he broke into professional ball he found himself limited to 100 pitches by the protective A's. Zito's work ethic is legendary.

"I work hard because I figure the quicker I get there," he said while still in the minor leagues, "the less I will have to catch up to people. I don't worry about the other guys, I can't get caught up in it. I don't lose sight of what I want, and I know what I need to do to work hard and have everything fall in place."

He worked with a nutritionist and a personal trainer—an Austrian bodybuilder who was such an "Arnold clone" it was scary—every day in the off-season at the legendary Gold's Gym ("the Mecca of bodybuilding") in L.A.'s Venice area. He gained weight but lost body fat after turning pro and put speed on his heater. At the 2000 SC alumni game, pitchers from both sides were getting tagged in a slugfest. Then Zito came in, and in one very

By the NUMBERS

17—The number of 20-game winners the Oakland A's had from 1968 to 2005:

1971: Vida Blue, Catfish Hunter

1972: Catfish Hunter

1973: Catfish Hunter, Vida Blue, Ken Holtzman

1974: Catfish Hunter

1975: Vida Blue

1980: Mike Norris

1987: Dave Stewart

1988: Dave Stewart

1989: Dave Stewart

1990: Bob Welch, Dave Stewart

2000: Tim Hudson

2001: Mark Mulder

2002: Barry Zito

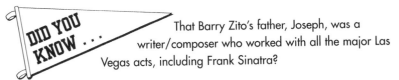

impressive inning he mowed down the side as if they had forgotten to bring their bats.

Zito was a kid who made you sit up and take notice, the kind you would mortgage the stadium to sign after watching him throw 20 pitches! That was the thinking of every general manager in baseball when he was coming up through the minor leagues. Beane probably had to hire extra secretaries to handle all the calls he got from other teams willing to take Zito off his hands. One possible trade almost went down: a blockbuster with the Angels involving Jim Edmonds. Although the details were not revealed, one can surmise that Zito was what the Angels wanted, and what the A's would not give up, even for a player like Edmonds.

Beane held on to Zito. Edmonds ended up leading St. Louis to the 2000 Central Division championship. The A's brought Zito along slowly. He pitched for the Sacramento River Cats and finally made the jump to Oakland late in 2000. Just in time.

Zito may have been just the spark the club needed to overtake Seattle by one half game to capture the West Division title. In the playoffs, Zito's inspired performance beating the vaunted Yankees in New York was one of the better coming-out parties in a long time.

"I always knew the A's didn't want to lose me," said Zito. Oakland's staff of Tim Hudson, Mark Mulder, and Zito reminded longtime Bay Area fans of the days of Catfish Hunter, Ken Holtzman, and Vida Blue.

"The A's had the best all-around minor league system in baseball my first year in the organization," said Barry. Two years later, many experts predicted they would be the team of the decade in the first 10 years of the new century.

"We have great coaching," said Zito of his minor league development. "Ron Romanick, formerly with Seattle, helped me a lot. So did the roving coaches, Curt Young, Glenn Abbott, and Pete Richert."

The 6'4", 205-pounder had his best year in 2002, when he was 23–5 with a 2.75 earned-run average. He beat Minnesota at the Metrodome in the playoffs and won the Cy Young Award.

Barry is a very nice, polite young man with Hollywood good looks. He was originally managed by Paul Cohen of TWC Management and has made forays into acting, with appearances on *Arli$$* and *The Chris Isaak Show*. He plays guitar with his sister's band and lives in the Hollywood Hills.

Barry has avoided injuries, unlike the great Bordley, allowing him to enjoy an excellent career. Watching this guy is always fun!

Miguel Tejada

The current success of the Oakland A's traces its beginnings to the Mark McGwire trade of 1997. Big Mac had befriended young Jason Giambi, getting him enthusiastic about lifting weights with him. Now we know that, although Giambi will not say, McGwire probably introduced him to steroids. We do know Giambi was juiced up and got the stuff from BALCO, the same Burlingame lab that handled Barry Bonds's supply. Whether an introduction came from McGwire, or with McGwire now in St. Louis Giambi needed to find a new source, is not clear.

The two Southern Californians bonded on and off the field. With McGwire's departure it became "Jason's team." But in 1997 another young Athletic made his debut. Miguel Tejada is another one of that endless line of phenomenal players from the Dominican Republic. Because they do not play in well-publicized American high school or college leagues and often sign while they are still children (some as young as 15 or 16), these players occasionally fly under the radar. Then all of a sudden we look up and there is a Miguel Tejada winning the MVP award.

Ben Grieve hit .312 in his September '97 call-up, then earned Rookie of the Year honors in 1998. The A's had nobody's attention going into 1999, but by late August Manager Art Howe was on *The Jim Rome Show,* his team being called "baseball's best story of the year" by the talk show host.

The 1999 A's indeed came out of nowhere to finish 87–75, good for second place, eight games behind Texas. It was in many ways similar to the 1969 A's, who at 88–74 finished nine games back of the veteran Twins.

All-Time Shortstops

1. Alex Rodriguez
2. Honus Wagner
3. Cal Ripken
4. Ernie Banks
5. Derek Jeter
6. **Miguel Tejada**
7. Nomar Garciaparra
8. Luis Aparicio
9. Luke Appling
10. Dave Concepcion

Players shown in bold played for the A's at some point in their careers.

Oakland closed to within a few games of Boston for a shot at the wild-card before fading in September, but they established themselves as clear favorites for 2000, a year in which they did win the division.

In 2000 Giambi was the marquee attraction in every way, earning the Most Valuable Player award, but Tejada was brilliant. He hit 30 home runs, drove in 115 (up from 84 in '99), and batted .275. He was excellent with the glove, durable (160 games)—a legit star.

That year baseball was in the middle of its "glory days" shortstop era. Never have so many great shortstops plied their trade at the same time. Alex Rodriguez of Seattle, Nomar Garciaparra of Boston, and Derek Jeter of the New York Yankees were each in their prime. Each player was media savvy and telegenic. Jeter and Garciaparra, in particular, fed off the intense Yankees–Red Sox rivalry and all that East Coast attention.

At that point, experts were saying that any of these three players could be considered the greatest shortstop of all time. It was a heady statement that may or may not hold up to scrutiny when examining the careers of Honus Wagner and Ernie Banks, but the combination of size, power, and defense was unprecedented. Aside from Banks, who became a first baseman after eight years, most shortstops in the past were wiry "good field, no hit" types. There was Phil Rizzuto, Dave Concepcion, Ozzie Smith, and Omar Vizquel. When Cal Ripken came along, he changed the dynamic of the position.

In the early 2000s, nobody mentioned Tejada with A-Rod, Jeter, or Nomar, but in Oakland they knew they had a man who was as valuable to the A's as those superstars were to their clubs.

In 2001 Miguel played all 162 games, hitting 31 homers with 113 runs batted in. In 2002 Tejada placed himself firmly in the discussion of great shortstops—not just in the decade but in history—when his

Miguel Tejada (left) was considered less heralded than such shortstop stars as Alex Rodriguez, Derek Jeter, and Nomar Garciaparra...until he won the 2002 AL MVP award. Photo courtesy of AP/Wide World Photos.

.308 average, accompanied by 34 home runs and 131 RBIs, earned him the Most Valuable Player award.

The A's again met with disappointment in the playoffs, but Tejada was an established star. In 2003 Tejada played out his contract with 27 home runs and 106 RBIs on the year. Beane was unable to get any compensation for him even though it was widely assumed he would become a free agent, because he was needed for the team's impressive run, which ended with an ignominious playoff loss to the Red Sox.

Unfortunately, Tejada went the way of free agency, which has not particularly worked out for him. He has continued to be a major star with the Baltimore Orioles, but that proud franchise has not contended for years. He is again under the radar while Jeter, now teamed with A-Rod at third base, continues to headline Broadway.

Oakland's ability to replace stars, whether they be Tim Hudson and Mark Mulder (with Joe Blanton, Dan Haren, and Rich Harden) or Miguel Tejada (with Bobby Crosby), has been nothing less than extraordinary. Billy Beane and his staff are pure wizards. Most fans do not realize how difficult it is to bring in that kind of quality, whether it be via the draft, via the farm system, or by trade. A short study of winning teams that lose the edge almost overnight—and the game is loaded with these kinds of teams—demonstrates Beane's great ability.

The really sad thing is that a player like Miguel was well liked by the fans and respected by the media. A long, mutually beneficial relationship would have been best for all concerned, but the game is just not the same as it once was.

TRIVIA

The Philadelphia-Oakland A's have 11 MVPs in their history. Which teams have more?

Answers to the trivia questions are on pages 196–198.

Boy Genius

Billy Beane is like the hand-picked successor to Julius Caesar, Octavian, who as a teenager was schooled in the ways of Roman politics, in many ways surpassing the older man, thus making his knowledge and wisdom indispensable. In so doing, Octavian made enemies out of jealous rivals. When Caesar was assassinated, his efforts at succeeding as emperor were eventually curtailed by those jealous rivals.

Beane's career as Oakland A's general manager has not been fraught with such peril, but Beane is the kind of guy who reads about people like Octavian, gleaning knowledge from politics and history, then actually using this knowledge in the running of a baseball team.

The old school thinks such lessons are malarkey, but the new breed have put their Ivy League degrees to use in building champions. Beane is very much of this new breed, a breed born out of the Alderson to La Russa success story. Its current members include Theo Epstein at Boston, J.P. Ricciardi at Toronto, and Beane.

On the surface, Beane does not appear to have the credentials of someone like the Harvard-educated Epstein. Beane is not a college man. He was a prep sensation coming out of San Diego but turned down a scholarship to Stanford to sign for big money with the New York Mets.

Although Beane did make it to the major leagues, he was never the star of early predictions. A top student, he always regretted turning down that Stanford education and has tried to make up for it by becoming a voracious reader of history, politics, biography—precisely the kind of books that detail the legend of Julius Caesar and Octavian.

General Manager Billy Beane (standing) is thought to be the most innovative baseball executive to come along since Branch Rickey. His methods have formed the new paradigm of diamond success.

Just as Caesar made sure Octavian knew the rules of Rome, so too did Sandy Alderson make sure Beane knew the ins and outs of being a general manager. Beane, the ex-player who came up as a scout, was taught more than just player evaluation.

"Sandy told me when I became his assistant that he wanted me negotiating contracts," Beane said. "A lot of general managers leave that for somebody else, but Sandy said with a small-market team, you always have to know how a contract will affect your team. You always have to be conscious of your payroll. So, I've always negotiated contracts."

Alderson recognized that a guy with no real formal education beyond high school had the wherewithal to learn something normally associated with lawyers like himself. Today, most assistant general managers are counted on for their contract skills, understanding the numbers, the caps, the rules, the union stipulations, and the budgetary concerns. Several have moved on to big jobs after training under Beane.

Michael Lewis's best-selling book *Moneyball* (2003) excruciatingly detailed how Beane was able to orchestrate complicated trades, such as the seven-player deal that brought Johnny Damon to the A's in 2001. The deal rubbed many the wrong way because, in essence, Beane outsmarted other general managers. He was like Bill Clinton, sharp enough to always know the end game, so no matter how complicated and troublesome it looked, he knew that when the dust settled he would come out ahead. Beane's Machiavellian baseball moves are rooted in his "game theory" models, developed from reading biographies of war leaders and the like.

Other GMs have been left holding the bag. The unwritten "old boys network" is one Beane does not wish to belong to. If he improves his team at the expense of embarrassing a colleague on a rival team, so be it. His strategy is born out of necessity. The A's are a small-market operation. They cannot afford to keep their superstars beyond their contract expiration.

Jason Giambi was lost after the 2001 season and Miguel Tejada after the 2003 campaign. In both cases, Beane had no choice. The team contended for a World Series berth right to the end, and these league MVPs were cogs in the machine. But Beane did trade Mark

All-Time General Managers

1. Branch Rickey
2. Buzzy Bavasi
3. **Charlie O. Finley**
4. George Weiss
5. Frank "the Trader" Lane
6. Paul Richards
7. Frank Cashen
8. **Billy Beane**
9. Bing Devine
10. Brian Cashman

General managers shown in bold headed the A's.

Mulder and Tim Hudson early, trying to get some quality in exchange for stars. He has made good use of the high draft picks Oakland gets when a player leaves for free agency and has stressed that money saved from high salaries be used for scouting and player development. In this regard, the A's have been very successful.

Beane has specific theories and rarely, if ever, veers from them. Like Connie Mack, he prefers the college player (Eddie Collins, Eddie Plank, Chief Bender). He uses himself as a good example, feeling that had he gone to Stanford instead of succumbing to New York's bonus, he not only would have grown as a man, getting the education he craved, but also would have improved as a player to the point where his career might have lived up to its original promise.

The A's have gone for high school players like Eric Chavez and Bobby Crosby and Latino stars like Tejada, but for the most part they like the college player, who tends to be better coached, smarter, media savvy, and more mature. Hudson went to Auburn. Mulder went to Michigan State. Barry Zito is a USC man. Jason Giambi came out of Cal State Long Beach. Mark Ellis: Florida. Mark Kotsay and Kirk Saarloos: Cal State Fullerton. Bobby Kielty: USC and Mississippi State. Huston Street: Texas. Nick Swisher: Ohio State. Eric Byrnes: UCLA. There are more examples.

Beane has taken some tepid criticism from those who see racism, or elitism, in his style. What Beane wants is a smart player with a good team attitude, not a clubhouse agitator. He wants a player who may be willing to re-sign with the club for less money (Mark Kotsay in 2005) instead of going for megamillions in the mercenary sweepstakes. The strategy makes sense on its face, but it has not worked 100 percent. Collegians such as Giambi went for the money, while other collegians such as Mulder and Hudson were traded because it was known that they would have, too.

Jeremy Bonderman was a first-round draft pick out of high school. Beane argued against picking such a young, inexperienced pitcher. Grady Fuson made that pick, and the resulting argument lead to Fuson's departure. Bonderman has been on the edge of stardom for several years.

Players like Swisher exemplify what Beane likes: college players from good families with baseball backgrounds, fundamentally sound, who have good eyes at the plate and take walks instead of chasing bad pitches. The Beane way is to work opposing hurlers into high pitch counts, take walks, and go for a big hit. His managers, Art Howe and Ken Macha, have had their personality clashes with Beane, but the station-to-station strategy seems to be the way of all of them. This has caused some criticism from those who argue that they should bunt,

TRIVIA

The New York Yankees are the greatest tradition in sports history with 26 world championships. Where do the A's rank?

Answers to the trivia questions are on pages 196–198.

steal, hit-and-run, and be more aggressive. The flip side to that is that this style can end rallies, wears players out over a long season, and causes injuries.

When Giambi, Jermaine Dye, and Tejada were hitting three-run home runs, the Beane-Howe-Macha strategy worked, but as these players have been lost to baseball economics, the team has been forced to adjust.

Beane's detractors have taken delight in the fact that his way, while consistently successful in the regular season, has not garnered for the team a World Series berth. There may be some truth to it, but

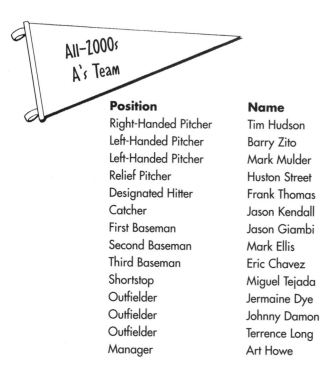

All-2000s
A's Team

Position	Name
Right-Handed Pitcher	Tim Hudson
Left-Handed Pitcher	Barry Zito
Left-Handed Pitcher	Mark Mulder
Relief Pitcher	Huston Street
Designated Hitter	Frank Thomas
Catcher	Jason Kendall
First Baseman	Jason Giambi
Second Baseman	Mark Ellis
Third Baseman	Eric Chavez
Shortstop	Miguel Tejada
Outfielder	Jermaine Dye
Outfielder	Johnny Damon
Outfielder	Terrence Long
Manager	Art Howe

in 2000, 2001, and 2003 the team failed in large part because of fluke plays, less so because of specific Beane ideas that were exposed as unworthy in October.

Oakland dropped a notch in 2004 and 2005, but they contended and have always provided excitement for their fans. Beane deserves credit for putting together a club, through trades and farm development, that has stayed competitive if not downright excellent despite the kind of changeover that annihilates most teams. His young charges of 2006–07 have all the appearance of future World Series contenders.

2005–2006:
A New Era

After the 2004 season, Billy Beane "allowed" Tim Hudson to go to Atlanta and Mark Mulder to go to St. Louis. Beane's judgment seems to have merit. Although both of these former Oakland aces have pitched effectively with their new teams, neither has approached his early 2000s level of excellence.

Barry Zito was retained. Although the tall southpaw lost some velocity on his fastball, becoming more of a finesse pitcher, he has been slightly better than the other two. His career as of this writing appears to have the potential for greater longevity and overall success.

In 2005 and 2006 many things stayed the same, but many things changed—for the most part, for the better. The heyday of Beane's A's was the Art Howe era (with emphasis on the powerhouse 2001 and 2002 teams). Ken Macha took over and carried the team into the 2003 postseason, again appearing to have all the tools necessary to win a world championship.

Year after year, the A's failed to deliver on their promise. A string of defeats in games in which the club had the opportunity to clinch a playoff series was disheartening, lasting from 2000 to 2004. In retrospect, the loss of Jason Giambi was a crushing blow, although his presence in the Yankees lineup has not produced expected results in the Bronx, either. The lesson of this decade has been that reaching the highest echelon of the sport, in the era of wild-cards and the two-playoff league postseason, is incredibly hard no matter how high the payroll.

Miguel Tejada's loss to free agency also hurt the A's, although he has not delivered Baltimore from its decade-long moribund state.

The Howe-Macha-Beane dilemma seems to be that they are built for regular-season success, possessing good moral fiber and leadership that results in strong finishes but lacking the kind of spectacular star power that delivered three titles in the 1970s and another in 1989.

Athletics pitcher Rich Harden and Tigers batter Craig Monroe watch the flight of Monroe's home run in Game 3 of the 2006 ALCS. Photo courtesy of AP/Wide World Photos.

The Reggie Jackson A's and the Bash Brothers argued among themselves and lacked the clubhouse camaraderie of the Beane bunch. Their success in comparison goes to show the relative unimportance of clubhouse unity.

Disappointment has marked the club, but they have maintained a level of regular-season competitiveness that must be attributed to the general manager. The 2005 team was extremely young. Shortstop Bobby Crosby, first baseman Dan Johnson, outfielder Nick Swisher, middle infielders Marco Scutaro and Mark Ellis, rookie reliever Huston Street, and young starters Rich Harden, Dan Haren, and Joe Blanton all performed very well.

Veterans in the form of outfielder Mark Kotsay and catcher Jason Kendall were welcome additions. The team's mainstays were Zito and third baseman Eric Chavez.

Over the course of two seasons, the prima donna Giants of Barry Bonds, playing in their showcase ballpark with all the bells and whistles of San Francisco glamour, fell inexorably by the side of the road while Oakland gave their loyal fans a truly exciting product.

TRIVIA

Where do the nine A's world championships rank among all other sports dynasties?

Answers to the trivia questions are on pages 196–198.

In 2005 the A's started out horribly. By the end of May it appeared that Beane had miscalculated and the club was headed for a period of doldrums. Perhaps the young pitchers possessed promise, but there was no hope held out for a successful '05 campaign. A brutal trip to Fenway Park resulted in a disheartening walk-off-home-run loss. Reliever Octavio Dotel seemed to be singing "Light My Fire" to hitters who salivated at his grooved, belt-high fastballs.

The A's gave up on Dotel and went with Street, who had pitched Texas to the 2002 College World Series title. For longtime A's fans, the summer of 2005 represented some of the most exciting hardball in the franchise's history. A spectacular run of success marked June, July, and August. In the end, the team peaked early. Anaheim captured the West when Oakland faltered down the stretch, but they were in it until the end, and nobody could complain.

In 2006 the A's entered the campaign favored to win the division. While there was no consensus that they would win the World Series (again, the Yankees on paper looked to be the best), there was certainly no lack of confidence.

The Boston Red Sox hit the wall and fell out of contention in late summer. Oakland stayed close enough throughout the early stages to strike when their inevitable late-season surge kicked into gear. It was a season in which good clubs failed to knock them off. The Angels lacked defense and succumbed in the West. The defending world champion White Sox lost a three-game series at home to the A's. Oakland rolled into Yankee Stadium and emerged with a sweep. The signs were all there.

For the second straight season, the A's were at times spectacular but seemed to weary toward the end. They held on to win the division with a 93–69 mark. Analyzing the club continued to be hard, at least offensively. The Beane method seems to produce wins, even runs, but not the gaudy statistics of the Yankees or even the Giants of a few years earlier.

Jay Payton had come over in a 2005 trade that resulted in popular local kid Eric Byrnes's departure. Payton proved a much better all-around player and in '05 batted .296, playing less spectacular but steadier defense than Byrnes had.

Kendall hit .295 while perfecting the art of tagging runners out at home plate. Milton Bradley's temper was corralled into a positive. He was great in the field while producing at the plate. Frank Thomas, considered washed up in Chicago, instead assured himself of Cooperstown while taking major strides toward the 500-homer mark. His near-MVP performance of 39 home runs with 114 runs batted in and a .270 average made the season. Beane was lucky or smart in acquiring Thomas for very little money. The record by now points to *smart*.

Scutaro was again steady. Swisher emerged as a power threat with 35 homers and 95 RBIs. Ellis did nothing until the last two months but made up for it with clutch hits to fuel winning streaks. Chavez played with a mysterious injury that curtailed his offensive production, but he elevated his defensive prowess to a level almost on par with Brooks Robinson and Graig Nettles from an earlier era.

All-Time
A's Team

Position	First Team	Second Team	Honorable Mention
Right-Handed Pitcher	Catfish Hunter	Dave Stewart	Tim Hudson
Right-Handed Pitcher	Chief Bender	George Earnshaw	
Left-Handed Pitcher	Lefty Grove	Barry Zito	Mark Mulder
Left-Handed Pitcher	Rube Waddell	Ken Holtzman	Bobby Shantz
Left-Handed Pitcher	Eddie Plank	Vida Blue	
Relief Pitcher	Dennis Eckersley	Huston Street	
Relief Pitcher	Rollie Fingers	Darold Knowles	
Catcher	Mickey Cochrane	Ray Fosse	
First Baseman	Jimmie Foxx	Mark McGwire	Jason Giambi
Second Baseman	Eddie Collins	Eddie Joost	
Third Baseman	Jimmy Dykes	Frank Baker	Sal Bando
Shortstop	Miguel Tejada	Jack Barry	Bert Campaneris
Outfielder	Rickey Henderson	Joe Rudi	Sam Chapman
Outfielder	Reggie Jackson	Gus Zernial	
Outfielder	Al Simmons	Jose Canseco	
Manager	Connie Mack	Dick Williams	Tony La Russa
Player	Jimmie Foxx		
Pitcher	Lefty Grove		

On the mound, Zito was the leader with a 16–10 mark to go with a 3.83 earned-run average. Pitching in his free agent year, Zito was good, but he has not yet answered the question: how good will he be? The 2002 Cy Young Award winner showed Hall of Fame potential from 2000 to 2002. There remains the distinct possibility that he will return to that level, but it is an uncertain possibility.

Joe Blanton was better pitching with little support in 2005 than with good support in 2006. He won 16 games, but his body type and propensity for beer poses a future challenge that he will either meet or succumb to. Stories of enormous bar tabs from his partying with Swisher on the road lend some question about both players' careers,

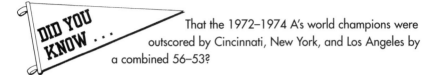

That the 1972–1974 A's world champions were outscored by Cincinnati, New York, and Los Angeles by a combined 56–53?

as both are talents in a game in which greatness goes to the rare ones who pay the highest cost. Mediocrity is the destiny of most.

Danny Haren was 14–13. Like several of his teammates, the discomfiting notion that only he stands between himself and greatness marked his second full year. Esteban Loaiza, a 20-game winner in Chicago (2003), was brought over. This move proved to be more of Beane's genius. Early on he was more "Lousy" than Loaiza, tossing batting practice floaters to be swatted about ballparks. He ran into off-field trouble and looked to be a lost cause.

It turned out he was hiding an injury but giving no excuses. Once healthy, he pitched well in the second half. The key to the year turned out to be Rich Harden. A young flame-thrower with a fastball in the high 90s, Harden was hurt. The old bugaboo of potential hung around his neck for another year, as it did for many of his teammates.

Justin Duchscherer was excellent in middle relief. Huston Street was good but not great. He had 37 saves, but his fastball was perceptibly flatter than the Longhorn star or the 2005 rookie phenom.

The playoffs opened in Minnesota, a "house of horrors" for Oakland over the years. About a month earlier they had imploded on the artificial turf, with the confusing same-color-as-the-ball roof. The Twins captured the Central on the last day of the season, meaning Oakland lost home-field advantage against a reeling Detroit squad. All the predictions were skewered over the next 10 days, though.

First, Zito pitched spectacularly in out-dueling Cy Young–winner Johan Santana, 3–2, behind Frank Thomas's key homer. Great defense by Kendall around home plate marked Oakland's three-game sweep.

Mark Kotsay hit an inside-the-park homer to power the 5–2 Game 2 win. In Oakland, Dan Haren won 8–3, and victory was theirs.

All seemed set, with Detroit coming in after upsetting the Yankees. Oakland had the home-field edge, the rotation right where they wanted it, and responded by getting swept. Zito set the pace by getting taken into long counts before getting blown out, and for all practical purposes that was the series.

Harden finally got his start after injuries and a couple of late-season rehab efforts, but it was too much to ask. Had he been healthy all year and into October, Oakland might have gone where the Tigers went instead. Detroit's young pitching staff of Nate Robertson, Jeremy Bonderman, and Justin Verlander, combined with veteran Kenny Rogers, suddenly resembled the 1954 Indians.

Milton Bradley summed up the season and in fact the whole Oakland approach over the years: "Everybody left it out on the field."

Page 157: The A's always scrambled to find a radio station, and with it a loyal audience. While the Giants have found a permanent home on KNBR, the A's have been all over the dial. After the great stars of the world champion teams left, Charlie O. Finley refused to pay for a major station, opting to have games carried by the University of California station. Cal student Larry Baer, now a top Giants exec, handled the microphone duties. The student signal did not carry much beyond Berkeley and could hardly be heard at the Coliseum itself.

Page 161: 11. Lefty Grove (1931), Jimmie Foxx (1932 and 1933), Bobby Shantz (1952), Vida Blue (1971), Reggie Jackson (1973), Jose Canseco (1988), Rickey Henderson (1990), Dennis Eckersley (1992), Jason Giambi (2000), and Miguel Tejada (2002)

Page 166: The Pacific 10 Conference with 11, followed by the Big Ten (10) and the SEC (0). Pac 10 Cy Young Award winners include USC's Tom Seaver, three (1969, '73, and '75); Randy Johnson, five (1995 and from 1999 to 2002); Barry Zito, one (2002); Stanford's Jim Lonborg, one (1967); and Jack McDowell, one (1993).

Page 171: The Pacific 10 Conference, previously known as the PCC and the Pac 8, has produced 12 MVPs. They include Jackie Jensen (1958) and Jeff Kent (2000) of California; Reggie Jackson (1973) and Barry Bonds (1990, '92, '93, 2001–04) of Arizona State; Fred Lynn (1975) of Southern California; and Jackie Robinson (1949) of UCLA. Tim Hudson's Auburn Tigers have produced the only two for the SEC: Frank Thomas (1993 and 1994). Mark Mulder's

Michigan State Spartans represent the Big Ten with their only two: Steve Garvey (1974) and Kirk Gibson (1988).

Page 182: The New York Yankees (19), the St. Louis Cardinals (15), and the New York–San Francisco Giants (12) have more MVPs in their history than the A's. The Brooklyn–Los Angeles Dodgers have 10. Boston has nine, Detroit eight.

Page 187: The A's are third in baseball with nine (1910, '11, '13, '29, '30, '72, '73, '74, '89). The Boston Pilgrims/Red Sox follow with six (1903, '12, '15, '16, '18, 2004). Next are the Giants (1905, '21, '22, '33, '54), Dodgers (1955, '63, '65, '81, '88), Pittsburgh Pirates (1909, '25, '60, '71, '79), and the Cincinnati Reds (1919, '40, '75, '76, '90) at five. The Detroit Tigers have four (1935, '45, '68, '84). The Baltimore Orioles (1966, '70, '83) and Chicago White Sox (1906, '17, 2005) have three. The Chicago Cubs have two (1907 and 1908).

Page 191: The A's rank eighth: USC has won 26 NCAA track championships; the Yankees have won 26 World Series. The Montreal Canadiens have won 24 Stanley Cups. The United States has been the medal leader in 17 Summer Olympic Games. The Boston Celtics have won 16 NBA titles. USC has won the College World Series 12 times; the Green Bay Packers have captured 12 NFL titles. USC and Notre Dame have won 11 national championships in football; UCLA has 11 NCAA basketball championships. The Cardinals have won 10 World Series and the A's nine. Since 1967, the Pittsburgh Steelers, San Francisco 49ers, and Dallas Cowboys have won five Super Bowls apiece.

Athletics
All-Time Roster
(through 2006 season)

Included players have appeared in at least one game for the A's. Players whose positions are indicated with a dash never played in the field and were used only as pinch-hitters, designated hitters, or pinch runners.

A

Andy Abad (1B)	2001
Glenn Abbott (P)	1973–76
Kurt Abbott (SS)	1993, 1998
Al Aber (P)	1957
Ted Abernathy (P)	1942–44
Merito Acosta (OF)	1918
Mark Acre (P)	1994–97
Dick Adams (1B)	1947
Mike Adams (OF)	1978
Willie Adams (P)	1918–19
Willie Adams (P)	1996–97
Dick Adkins (SS)	1942
Troy Afenir (C)	1990–91
Jack Aker (P)	1964–68
Darrel Akerfelds (P)	1986
Mike Aldrete (OF)	1993–95
Gary Alexander (C)	1978
Matt Alexander (OF)	1975–77
Bob Allen (OF)	1919
Dick Allen (1B)	1977
Dana Allison (P)	1991
Bill Almon (SS)	1983–84
Felipe Alou (OF)	1970–71
Jesus Alou (OF)	1973–74
Matty Alou (OF)	1972

Dell Alston (OF)	1978
George Alusik (OF)	1962–64
Brant Alyea (OF)	1972
Wayne Ambler (SS)	1937–39
Walter Ancker (P)	1915
Dwain Anderson (SS)	1971–72
Walter Anderson (P)	1917–19
Elbert Andrews (P)	1925
Mike Andrews (2B)	1973
Joaquin Andujar (P)	1986–87
Kevin Appier (P)	1999–2000
Fred Applegate (P)	1904
Fred Archer (P)	1936–37
Jim Archer (P)	1961–62
Marcos Armas (1B)	1993
Tony Armas (OF)	1977–82
Harry Armbruster (OF)	1906
George Armstrong (C)	1946
Howard Armstrong (P)	1911
Larry Arndt (1B)	1989
Orie Arntzen (P)	1943
Fernando Arroyo (P)	1982–86
Joe Astroth (C)	1945–56
Keith Atherton (P)	1983–86
Tommy Atkins (P)	1909–10
Joe Azcue (C)	1962–63

B

Loren Babe (3B)	1953
Johnny Babich (P)	1940–41
Shooty Babitt (2B)	1981

Eddie Bacon (P)	1917	Bill Beckmann (P)	1939–42
Bill Bagwell (OF)	1925	Todd Belitz (P)	2000
Stan Bahnsen (P)	1975–77	Kevin Bell (3B)	1982
Gene Bailey (OF)	1917	Zeke Bella (OF)	1959
Harold Baines (DH)	1990–92	Mark Bellhorn (2B)	1997–98, 2000–01
Doug Bair (P)	1977, 1986	Chief Bender (P)	1903–14
Bock Baker (P)	1901	Vern Benson (3B)	1943–46
Dusty Baker (OF)	1985–86	Al Benton (P)	1934–35
Frank Baker (3B)	1908–14	Johnny Berger (C)	1922
Neal Baker (P)	1927	Tony Bernazard (2B)	1987
Scott Baker (P)	1995	Bill Bernhard (P)	1901–02
Steve Baker (P)	1982–83	Geronimo Berroa (DH)	1994–97
Chris Bando (C)	1989	Charlie Berry (C)	1925, 1934–38
Sal Bando (3B)	1966–76	Claude Berry (C)	1906–07
Everett Bankston (OF)	1915	Joe Berry (P)	1944–46
Dave Barbee (OF)	1926	Reno Bertoia (3B)	1961
Babe Barna (OF)	1937–38	Herman Besse (P)	1940–46
Scotty Barr (OF)	1908–09	Jeff Bettendorf (P)	1984
Bill Barrett (OF)	1921	Hal Bevan (3B)	1952, 1955
Dick Barrett (P)	1933	Hank Biasatti (1B)	1949
Hardin Barry (P)	1912	Lyle Bigbee (P)	1920
Jack Barry (SS)	1908–15	George Binks (OF)	1947–48
John Barthold (P)	1904	Tim Birtsas (P)	1985–86
Bill Bartley (P)	1906–07	Bill Bishop (P)	1921
Irv Bartling (SS)	1938	Charlie Bishop (P)	1952–55
Daric Barton (1B)	2006	Max Bishop (2B)	1924–33
Harry Barton (C)	1905	Joe Bitker (P)	1990
Norm Bass (P)	1961–63	Don Black (P)	1943–45
Charlie Bates (OF)	1927	Ewell Blackwell (P)	1955
Ray Bates (3B)	1917	George Blaeholder (P)	1935
Bill Bathe (C)	1986	Buddy Blair (3B)	1942
Tony Batista (3B)	1996–97	Ed Blake (P)	1957
Allen Battle (OF)	1996	Johnny Blanchard (OF)	1965
Chris Batton (P)	1976	Gil Blanco (P)	1966
Hank Bauer (OF)	1960–61	Lance Blankenship (OF)	1988–93
Lou Bauer (P)	1918	Joe Blanton (P)	2004–06
Stan Baumgartner (P)	1924–26	Don Blasingame (2B)	1966
Mike Baxes (SS)	1956–58	Curt Blefary (OF)	1971–72
Don Baylor (DH)	1976, 1988	Ray Blemker (P)	1960
Billy Beane (OF)	1989	Mike Blowers (3B)	1998
Dave Beard (P)	1980–83	Bert Blue (C)	1908
Rich Becker (OF)	1999–2000	Vida Blue (P)	1969–77

Chet Boak (2B)	1960	John Briggs (P)	1960
Charlie Boardman (P)	1913–14	John Briscoe (P)	1991–96
Hiram Bocachica (OF)	2005–06	Lou Brissie (P)	1947–51
Bruce Bochte (1B)	1984–86	Tilson Brito (2B)	1997
Ping Bodie (OF)	1917	Pete Broberg (P)	1978
Joe Boever (P)	1993	Bobby Brooks (OF)	1969–72
Warren Bogle (P)	1968	Scott Brosius (3B)	1991–97
Pat Bohen (P)	1913	Art Brouthers (3B)	1906
Joe Boley (SS)	1927–32	Boardwalk Brown (P)	1911–14
Don Bollweg (1B)	1954–55	Darrell Brown (OF)	1982
Frank Bonner (2B)	1902	Jeremy Brown (C)	2006
Dan Boone (P)	1919	Jim Brown (OF)	1916
Ray Boone (3B)	1959	Larry Brown (SS)	1971–72
Rich Bordi (P)	1980–81, 1988	Norm Brown (P)	1943–46
Mike Bordick (SS)	1990–96	Ollie Brown (OF)	1972
Rick Bosetti (OF)	1981–82	Jerry Browne (2B)	1992–93
Dick Bosman (P)	1975–76	Lou Bruce (OF)	1904
Henry Bostick (3B)	1915	Earle Brucker (C)	1937–43, 1948
Rafael Bournigal (SS)	1996–98	Frank Bruggy (C)	1922–24
Pat Bourque (1B)	1973–74	Mike Brumley (SS)	1994
Jim Bowie (1B)	1994	George Brunet (P)	1956–60
Micah Bowie (P)	2002–03	Billy Bryan (C)	1961–66
Charlie Bowles (P)	1943–45	Derek Bryant (OF)	1979
Weldon Bowlin (3B)	1967	Mark Budaska (DH)	1978–81
Joe Bowman (P)	1932	Red Bullock (P)	1936
Ted Bowsfield (P)	1963–64	Tom Burgmeier (P)	1983–84
Bob Boyd (1B)	1961	Bill Burgo (OF)	1943–44
Clete Boyer (3B)	1955–57	Glenn Burke (OF)	1978–79
Cloyd Boyer (P)	1955	Wally Burnette (P)	1956–58
Bill Bradford (P)	1956	Dennis Burns (P)	1923–24
Chad Bradford (P)	2001–04	George Burns (1B)	1918–20, 1929
Bert Bradley (P)	1983	Joe Burns (3B)	1944–45
Milton Bradley (OF)	2006	Todd Burns (P)	1988–91
Dallas Bradshaw (2B)	1917	Ray Burris (P)	1984
Al Brancato (SS)	1939–45	Jeff Burroughs (OF)	1982–84
Dud Branom (1B)	1927	John Burrows (P)	1943
Marshall Brant (1B)	1983	Dick Burrus (1B)	1919–20
Frank Brazill (1B)	1921–22	Moe Burtschy (P)	1950–56
Bill Breckinridge (P)	1929	Ed Busch (SS)	1943–45
Rube Bressler (OF)	1914–16	Don Buschhorn (P)	1965
Billy Brewer (P)	1997	Joe Bush (P)	1912–17, 1928
George Brickley (OF)	1913	Ralph Buxton (P)	1938

Freddie Bynum (OF)	2005	Bob Cerv (OF)	1957–60
Harry Byrd (P)	1950–53	Ron Cey (3B)	1987
Eric Byrnes (OF)	2000–05	Dave Chalk (3B)	1979
Jim Byrnes (C)	1906	Charlie Chant (OF)	1975
		Fred Chapman (SS)	1939–41
C		John Chapman (SS)	1924
Greg Cadaret (P)	1987–89	Sam Chapman (OF)	1938–51
Sugar Cain (P)	1932–35	Ed Charles (3B)	1962–67
Kiko Calero (P)	2005–06	Ossie Chavarria (2B)	1966–67
Fred Caligiuri (P)	1941–42	Eric Chavez (3B)	1998–2006
Ben Callahan (P)	1983	Harry Chiti (C)	1958–60
Frank Callaway (SS)	1921–22	Steve Chitren (P)	1990–91
Ernie Camacho (P)	1980	Bobby Chouinard (P)	1996
Bert Campaneris (SS)	1964–76	Ryan Christenson (OF)	1998–2001
Kevin Campbell (P)	1991–93	Russ Christopher (P)	1942–47
Tom Candiotti (P)	1998–99	Darryl Cias (C)	1983
Jose Canseco (OF)	1985–92, 1997	Joe Cicero (OF)	1945
Ozzie Canseco (OF)	1990	Ed Cihocki (SS)	1932–33
Guy Cantrell (P)	1927	Gino Cimoli (OF)	1962–64
Andy Carey (3B)	1960–61	Lou Ciola (P)	1943
Charlie Carr (1B)	1901	Frank Cipriani (OF)	1961
Chico Carrasquel (SS)	1958	Bill Cissell (2B)	1937
Doc Carroll (C)	1916	Allie Clark (OF)	1951–53
Tom Carroll (3B)	1959	Doug Clark (OF)	2006
Nick Carter (P)	1908	Jermaine Clark (OF)	2005
Sol Carter (P)	1931	Ron Clark (3B)	1971–72
Rico Carty (OF)	1973, 1978	Gowell Claset (P)	1933
Joe Cascarella (P)	1934–35	Lou Clinton (OF)	1965
Santiago Casilla (P)	2004–06	Tom Clyde (P)	1943
George Caster (P)	1934–40	Andy Coakley (P)	1902–06
Jim Castiglia (C)	1942	Ty Cobb (OF)	1927–28
Alberto Castillo (C)	2005	Mickey Cochrane (C)	1925–33
Luis Castro (2B)	1902	Chris Codiroli (P)	1982–87
Ramon Castro (3B)	2004	Mike Colangelo (OF)	2002
Danny Cater (1B)	1966–69	Rocky Colavito (OF)	1964
Bill Caudill (P)	1984, 1987	Nate Colbert (1B)	1976
Jake Caulfield (SS)	1946	Ed Coleman (OF)	1932–35
Wayne Causey (SS)	1961–66	Joe Coleman (P)	1942–53
Art Ceccarelli (P)	1955–56	Joe Coleman (P)	1977–78
Domingo Cedeno (2B)	1998–99	Ray Coleman (OF)	1948
Orlando Cepeda (1B)	1972	Rip Coleman (P)	1957, 1959

Allan Collamore (P)	1911	Cap Crowell (P)	1915–16
Dave Collins (OF)	1985	Woody Crowson (P)	1945
Eddie Collins (2B)	1906–14, 1927–30	Press Cruthers (2B)	1913–14
Eddie Collins (OF)	1939–42	Fausto Cruz (SS)	1994–95
Jimmy Collins (3B)	1907–08	Juan Cruz (P)	2005
Zip Collins (OF)	1921	Tim Cullen (2B)	1972
Bob Cone (P)	1915	Dick Culler (SS)	1936
Billy Conigliaro (OF)	1973	Mike Cunningham (P)	1906
Bill Connelly (P)	1945	Jim Curry (2B)	1909
Steve Connelly (P)	1998		
Bill Conroy (C)	1935–37	**D**	
Tim Conroy (P)	1978–85	John D'Acquisto (P)	1982
Billy Consolo (SS)	1962	Bud Daley (P)	1958–61
Owen Conway (3B)	1915	Pete Daley (C)	1960
Bobby Coombs (P)	1933	Tom Daley (OF)	1913–14
Jack Coombs (P)	1906–14	Bert Daly (2B)	1903
Pat Cooper (P)	1946–47	Johnny Damon (OF)	2001
Rocky Coppinger (P)	2001–02	Harry Damrau (3B)	1915
Art Corcoran (3B)	1915	Art Daney (P)	1928
Jim Corsi (P)	1988–89	Dave Danforth (P)	1911–12
Jim Corsi (P)	1992, 1995–96	Buck Danner (SS)	1915
Ray Cosey (—)	1980	Ron Darling (P)	1991–95
Ensign Cottrell (P)	1913	Vic Davalillo (OF)	1973–74
Marlan Coughtry (2B)	1962	Claude Davidson (2B)	1918
Clint Courtney (C)	1961	Chick Davies (P)	1914–15
Stan Coveleski (P)	1912	Bob Davis (P)	1958–60
Wes Covington (OF)	1961	Bud Davis (P)	1915
Glenn Cox (P)	1955–58	Crash Davis (2B)	1940–42
Jeff Cox (2B)	1980–81	Harry Davis (1B)	1901–11, 1913–17
Toots Coyne (3B)	1914	Mike Davis (OF)	1980–87
Roy Crabb (P)	1912	Storm Davis (P)	1987–89, 1993
Walt Craddock (P)	1955–58	Tod Davis (SS)	1949–51
George Craig (P)	1907	Tommy Davis (OF)	1970–71
Doc Cramer (OF)	1929–35	Bill Dawley (P)	1989
Sam Crane (SS)	1914–16	Chubby Dean (P)	1936–41
Willie Crawford (OF)	1977	Bobby Del Greco (OF)	1961–63
Jack Crimian (P)	1956	Jim Delsing (OF)	1960
Jim Cronin (2B)	1929	Joe DeMaestri (SS)	1953–59
Bobby Crosby (SS)	2003–06	Billy DeMars (SS)	1948
Lave Cross (3B)	1901–05	Claud Derrick (SS)	1910–12
Monte Cross (SS)	1902–07	Russ Derry (OF)	1946

Jeremy Giambi (OF)	2000–02	Al Grunwald (P)	1959
Charlie Gibson (C)	1924	Joe Grzenda (P)	1964–66
Joe Giebel (C)	1913	Mike Guerra (C)	1947–50
Paul Giel (P)	1961	Mario Guerrero (SS)	1978–80
Bob Giggie (P)	1960, 1962	Jose Guillen (OF)	2003
Joe Ginsberg (C)	1956	Ben Guintini (OF)	1950
Keith Ginter (2B)	2005	Randy Gumpert (P)	1936–38
Tommy Giordano (2B)	1953	Mark Guthrie (P)	2001
Dave Giusti (P)	1977	Johnny Guzman (P)	1991–92
Tom Glass (P)	1925		
Ryan Glynn (P)	2005	**H**	
Orlando Gonzalez (1B)	1980	Bruno Haas (P)	1915
Lee Gooch (OF)	1917	Moose Haas (P)	1986–87
Danny Goodwin (DH)	1982	Mule Haas (OF)	1928–32, 1938
Tom Gorman (P)	1955–59	Bump Hadley (P)	1941
Jim Gosger (OF)	1966–68	Kent Hadley (1B)	1958–59
Rich Gossage (P)	1992–93	Bill Haeffner (C)	1915
Billy Grabarkewitz (3B)	1975	John Halama (P)	2003
Jason Grabowski (OF)	2002–03	Sammy Hale (3B)	1923–29
Milt Graff (2B)	1957–58	Ray Haley (C)	1916–17
Mudcat Grant (P)	1970–71	Dick Hall (P)	1960
Dolly Gray (P)	1924–27	Irv Hall (2B)	1943–46
Johnny Gray (P)	1954–55	Brad Halsey (P)	2006
Dick Green (2B)	1963–74	Dave Hamilton (P)	1972–75, 1979–80
Joe Green (—)	1924	Tom Hamilton (1B)	1952–53
Vean Gregg (P)	1918	Ken Hamlin (SS)	1960
Bill Grevell (P)	1919	Luke Hamlin (P)	1944
Ben Grieve (OF)	1997–2000	Chris Hammond (P)	2004
Lee Griffeth (P)	1946	Granny Hamner (SS)	1962
Alfredo Griffin (SS)	1985–87	Buddy Hancken (C)	1940
Ivy Griffin (1B)	1919–21	Garry Hancock (OF)	1983–84
Pug Griffin (1B)	1917	Gene Handley (2B)	1946–47
Guido Grilli (P)	1966	Vern Handrahan (P)	1964–66
Bob Grim (P)	1958–59, 1962	Larry Haney (C)	1969–73, 1974–76
Oscar Grimes (3B)	1946	Jay Hankins (OF)	1961–63
Charlie Grimm (1B)	1916	Preston Hanna (P)	1982
Lew Groh (3B)	1919	Jack Hannifin (3B)	1906
Buddy Groom (P)	1996–99	Aaron Harang (P)	2002–03
Wayne Gross (3B)	1976–83, 1986	Rich Harden (P)	2003–06
Johnny Groth (OF)	1956–57	Dan Haren (P)	2005–06
Lefty Grove (P)	1925–33	Tim Harikkala (P)	2005
Roy Grover (2B)	1916–19	Mike Harkey (P)	1995

Brian Harper (C)	1987, 1995	Weldon Henley (P)	1903–05
Jack Harper (P)	1915	Ray Herbert (P)	1955–61
Tommy Harper (OF)	1975	Gil Heredia (P)	1998–2001
Slim Harrell (P)	1912	Ramon Hernandez (C)	1999–2003
Ken Harrelson (1B)	1963–67	Jose Herrera (OF)	1995–96
Bill Harrington (P)	1953, 1955–56	Troy Herriage (P)	1956
Bob Harris (P)	1942	Mike Hershberger (OF)	1965–69
Bubba Harris (P)	1948–49, 1951	Whitey Herzog (OF)	1958–60
Lum Harris (P)	1941–46	George Hesselbacher (P)	1916
Reggie Harris (P)	1990–91	Ed Heusser (P)	1940
Spencer Harris (OF)	1930	Johnnie Heving (C)	1931–32
Tom Harrison (P)	1965	Jesse Hickman (P)	1965–66
Slim Harriss (P)	1920–26	Pinky Higgins (3B)	1930–36
Topsy Hartsel (OF)	1902–11	Charlie High (OF)	1919–20
Chad Harville (P)	1999, 2001, 2003–04	Erik Hiljus (P)	2001–02
Ron Hassey (C)	1988–90	Dave Hill (P)	1957
Joe Hassler (SS)	1928–29	Donnie Hill (2B)	1983–86
Gene Hasson (1B)	1937–38	Jesse Hill (OF)	1937
Bob Hasty (P)	1919–24	Red Hill (P)	1917
Scott Hatteberg (1B)	2002–05	Shawn Hillegas (P)	1992–93
Gary Haught (P)	1997	Ed Hilley (3B)	1903
Joe Hauser (1B)	1922–28	A.J. Hinch (C)	1998–2000
Clem Hausmann (P)	1949	Billy Hitchcock (3B)	1950–52
Andy Hawkins (P)	1991	Danny Hoffman (OF)	1903–06
Jack Hayden (OF)	1901	Willie Hogan (OF)	1911
Frankie Hayes (C)	1933–42, 1944–45	Wally Holborow (P)	1948
Jimmy Haynes (P)	1997–99	Chick Holmes (P)	1918
Thomas Healy (3B)	1915–16	Jim Holmes (P)	1906
Mike Heath (C)	1979–85	Jim Holt (OF)	1974–76
Dave Heaverlo (P)	1978–79, 1981	Red Holt (1B)	1925
Don Heffner (2B)	1943	Mike Holtz (P)	2002
Mike Hegan (1B)	1971–73	Ken Holtzman (P)	1972–75
Fred Heimach (P)	1920–26	Mark Holzemer (P)	1998–99
Gorman Heimueller (P)	1983–84	Rick Honeycutt (P)	1987–93, 1995
Heinie Heitmuller (OF)	1909–10	Alex Hooks (1B)	1935
Woodie Held (SS)	1957–58	Bob Hooper (P)	1950–52
Eric Helfand (C)	1993–95	Leon Hooten (P)	1974
Scott Hemond (C)	1989–94	Sam Hope (P)	1907
Dave Henderson (OF)	1988–93	Don Hopkins (DH)	1975–76
Rickey Henderson (OF)	1979–84, 1989–95, 1998	Joe Horlen (P)	1972
Steve Henderson (OF)	1985–87	Vince Horsman (P)	1992–94
George Hendrick (OF)	1971–72	Willie Horton (OF)	1978

Tim Hosley (C)	1973–74, 1976–78, 1981
Gene Host (P)	1957
Byron Houck (P)	1912–14
Frank House (C)	1958–59
Ben Houser (1B)	1910
Steve Hovley (OF)	1970–71
Steve Howard (OF)	1990
Jay Howell (P)	1985–87
Dann Howitt (OF)	1989–92
Dick Howser (SS)	1961–63
Tex Hoyle (P)	1952
Waite Hoyt (P)	1931
Glenn Hubbard (2B)	1988–89
Earl Huckleberry (P)	1935
Dave Hudgens (1B)	1983
Tim Hudson (P)	1999–2004
Hank Hulvey (P)	1923
Billy Hunter (SS)	1957–58
Catfish Hunter (P)	1965–74
Carl Husta (SS)	1925
Bert Husting (P)	1902
Warren Huston (3B)	1937

I

Jason Isringhausen (P)	1999–2001

J

Ray Jablonski (3B)	1959–60
Joe Jackson (OF)	1908–09
Reggie Jackson (OF)	1968–75, 1987
Spook Jacobs (2B)	1954–56
Baby Doll Jacobson (OF)	1927
Brook Jacoby (3B)	1991
John Jaha (1B)	1999–2001
Charlie Jamieson (OF)	1917–18
Kevin Jarvis (P)	1999
Stan Javier (OF)	1986–90, 1994–95
Tom Jenkins (OF)	1926
Doug Jennings (OF)	1988–91
Robin Jennings (OF)	2001
Willie Jensen (P)	1914
D'Angelo Jimenez (IF)	2006

Manny Jimenez (OF)	1962–66
Miguel Jimenez (P)	1993–94
Tommy John (P)	1985
Doug Johns (P)	1995–96, 2000
Bill Johnson (OF)	1916–17
Bob Johnson (OF)	1933–42
Bob Johnson (SS)	1960, 1969–70
Cliff Johnson (DH)	1981–82
Dan Johnson (1B)	2005–06
Dane Johnson (P)	1997
Deron Johnson (1B)	1961–62, 1973–74
Hank Johnson (P)	1936
Jing Johnson (P)	1916–28
John Henry Johnson (P)	1978–79
Ken Johnson (P)	1958–61
Mark Johnson (C)	2003
Paul Johnson (OF)	1920–21
Rankin Johnson (P)	1941
Roy Johnson (P)	1918
Stan Johnson (OF)	1961
Walt Johnson (P)	1917
Doc Johnston (1B)	1922
Jay Johnstone (OF)	1973
John Johnstone (P)	1997
Doug Jones (P)	1999–2000
Gordon Jones (P)	1962
Jeff Jones (P)	1980–84
John Jones (OF)	1923–32
Marcus Jones (P)	2000
Eddie Joost (SS)	1947–54
Mike Jorgensen (1B)	1977
Felix Jose (OF)	1988–90
Rick Joseph (3B)	1964
Bob Joyce (P)	1939
Dick Joyce (P)	1965
Ed Jurak (SS)	1988
David Justice (OF)	2002

K

Jeff Kaiser (P)	1985
John Kalahan (C)	1903

Bill Kalfass (P)	1937	Ernie Kish (OF)	1945
Eric Karros (1B)	2004	Lou Klein (2B)	1951
Steve Karsay (P)	1993–94, 1997, 2006	Ed Klieman (P)	1950
Bob Kearney (C)	1981–83	Lou Klimchock (3B)	1958–61
Teddy Kearns (1B)	1920	Ron Klimkowski (P)	1971
Dave Keefe (P)	1917–21	Bob Kline (P)	1934
Ed Keegan (P)	1961	Joe Klink (P)	1990–91
Vic Keen (P)	1918	Mickey Klutts (3B)	1979–82
Jim Keesey (1B)	1925–30	Lou Knerr (P)	1945–46
Randy Keisler (P)	2006	Austin Knickerbocker (OF)	1947
George Kell (3B)	1943–46	Bill Knickerbocker (SS)	1942
Skeeter Kell (2B)	1952	John Knight (SS)	1905–07
Al Kellett (P)	1923	Jack Knott (P)	1941–46
Harry Kelley (P)	1936–38	Darold Knowles (P)	1971–74
Alex Kellner (P)	1948–58	Tom Knowlson (P)	1915
Walt Kellner (P)	1952–53	Bill Knowlton (P)	1920
Al Kellogg (P)	1908	Billy Koch (P)	2002
Bill Kelly (1B)	1920	Don Kolloway (2B)	1953
Ren Kelly (P)	1923	Shane Komine (P)	2006
Jason Kendall (C)	2005–06	Brad Komminsk (OF)	1991
Ed Kenna (P)	1902	Bruce Konopka (1B)	1942–46
Joe Kennedy (P)	2005–06	Graham Koonce (1B)	2003
Joe Keough (OF)	1968	Larry Kopf (SS)	1914–15
Matt Keough (P)	1977–83	Merlin Kopp (OF)	1918–19
Gus Keriazakos (P)	1955	Mark Kotsay (OF)	2004–06
Bill Kern (OF)	1962	Harry Krause (P)	1908–12
Fred Ketchum (OF)	1901	Lew Krausse (P)	1931–32
Gus Ketchum (P)	1922	Lew Krausse (P)	1961–69
Steve Kiefer (3B)	1984–85	Danny Kravitz (C)	1960
Bobby Kielty (OF)	2004–06	Mike Kreevich (OF)	1942
Leo Kiely (P)	1960	Lou Kretlow (P)	1956
Mike Kilkenny (P)	1972	Bill Krueger (P)	1983–87
Evans Killeen (P)	1959	Dick Kryhoski (1B)	1955
Lee King (OF)	1916	Ted Kubiak (2B)	1967–69, 1972–75
Mike Kingery (OF)	1992	Tim Kubinski (P)	1997, 1999
Brian Kingman (P)	1979–82	Johnny Kucab (P)	1950–52
Dave Kingman (OF)	1984–86	Johnny Kucks (P)	1959–60
Dennis Kinney (P)	1982	Bert Kuczynski (P)	1943
Walt Kinney (P)	1919–23	John Kull (P)	1909
Mike Kircher (P)	1919	Mike Kume (P)	1955
Bill Kirk (P)	1961	Bill Kunkel (P)	1961–62
Tom Kirk (—)	1947	Marty Kutyna (P)	1959–60

A's Essential

L

Chet Laabs (OF)	1947
Bob Lacey (P)	1977–80
Marcel Lachemann (P)	1969–71
Rene Lachemann (C)	1965–66, 1968
Ed Lagger (P)	1934
Nap Lajoie (2B)	1901–02, 1915–16
Bill Lamar (OF)	1924–27
Dennis Lamp (P)	1987
Bill Landis (P)	1963
Jim Landis (OF)	1965
Rick Langford (P)	1977–86
Red Lanning (OF)	1916
Carney Lansford (3B)	1983–92
Jack Lapp (C)	1908–15
Ed Larkin (C)	1909
Don Larsen (P)	1960–61
Tony La Russa (2B)	1963, 1968–71
Tom Lasorda (P)	1956
Charlie Lau (C)	1963–64
Billy Lauder (3B)	1901
George Lauzerique (P)	1967–69
Doc Lavan (SS)	1913
Gary Lavelle (P)	1987
Vance Law (3B)	1991
Otis Lawry (2B)	1916–17
Brett Laxton (P)	1999
Tom Leahy (C)	1901
Fred Lear (3B)	1915
Bevo Lebourveau (OF)	1929
Paul Lehner (OF)	1950–51
Justin Lehr (P)	2004
Dave Leiper (P)	1984, 1986–87, 1994–95
Dummy Leitner (P)	1901
Johnnie LeMaster (SS)	1987
Patrick Lennon (OF)	1997
Ed Lennox (3B)	1906
Elmer Leonard (P)	1911
John Leovich (C)	1941
Brian Lesher (OF)	1996–98
Allan Lewis (OF)	1967–70, 1972–73
Darren Lewis (OF)	1990
Richie Lewis (P)	1997
Cory Lidle (P)	2001–02
Dutch Lieber (P)	1935–36
Glenn Liebhardt (P)	1930
Bill Lillard (SS)	1939–40
Ted Lilly (P)	2002–03
Lou Limmer (1B)	1951–54
Paul Lindblad (P)	1965–71, 1973–76
Bob Lindemann (OF)	1901
Axel Lindstrom (P)	1916
Larry Lintz (2B)	1976–77
Hod Lisenbee (P)	1936
Jack Littrell (SS)	1952–55
Paddy Livingston (C)	1909–11
Esteban Loaiza (P)	2005–06
Harry Lochhead (SS)	1901
Bob Locker (P)	1970–72
Skip Lockwood (P)	1965
Dario Lodigiani (3B)	1938–40
Lep Long (P)	1911
Terrence Long (OF)	1999–2003
Pete Loos (P)	1901
Davey Lopes (2B)	1982–84
Hector Lopez (OF)	1955–59
Bris Lord (OF)	1905–07, 1910–12
Andrew Lorraine (P)	1997
Pete Lovrich (P)	1963
Torey Lovullo (2B)	1996
Sam Lowry (P)	1942–43
Hal Luby (3B)	1936
Eric Ludwick (P)	1997
Jerry Lumpe (2B)	1959–63
Scott Lydy (OF)	1993
Rick Lysander (P)	1980

M

Duke Maas (P)	1958
John Mabry (OF)	2002
Mike Macfarlane (C)	1998–99
Earle Mack (1B)	1910–14
Shane Mack (OF)	1998

Eric Mackenzie (C)	1955	Cloy Mattox (C)	1929
Gordon Mackenzie (C)	1961	Harry Matuzak (P)	1934–36
Felix Mackiewicz (OF)	1941–43	Carmen Mauro (OF)	1953
John Mackinson (P)	1953	Dal Maxvill (SS)	1972–75
Ed Madjeski (C)	1932–34	Bert Maxwell (P)	1908
Dave Magadan (3B)	1997–98	Brent Mayne (C)	1997
Harl Maggert (OF)	1912	Eddie Mayo (2B)	1943
Mike Magnante (P)	2000–02	Wickey McAvoy (C)	1913–19
Roy Mahaffey (P)	1930–35	Bill McCahan (P)	1946–49
Ron Mahay (P)	1999–2000	Emmett McCann (SS)	1920–21
Al Mahon (P)	1930	David McCarty (1B)	2003
Emil Mailho (OF)	1936	Steve McCatty (P)	1977–85
Jim Mains (P)	1943	Sam McConnell (3B)	1915
Hank Majeski (3B)	1946–49, 1951–52	Barney McCosky (OF)	1946–51
Ben Mallonee (OF)	1921	Willie McCovey (1B)	1976
Sheldon Mallory (OF)	1977	Benny McCoy (2B)	1940–41
Lew Malone (3B)	1915–16	Les McCrabb (P)	1939–50
Angel Mangual (OF)	1971–76	Frank McCue (3B)	1922
Fred Manrique (2B)	1991	Mickey McDermott (P)	1957, 1961
Frank Manush (3B)	1908	Danny McDevitt (P)	1962
Phil Marchildon (P)	1940–49	Hank McDonald (P)	1931–33
Johnny Marcum (P)	1933–35	Jason McDonald (OF)	1997–99
Roger Maris (OF)	1958–59	Lee McElwee (3B)	1916
Gene Markland (2B)	1950	Willie McGee (OF)	1990
Gonzalo Marquez (1B)	1972–73	Conny McGeehan (P)	1903
Billy Martin (2B)	1957	Bill McGhee (1B)	1944–45
Doc Martin (P)	1908–12	Ed McGhee (OF)	1953–54
Morrie Martin (P)	1951–54	John McGillen (P)	1944
Pat Martin (P)	1919–20	Beauty McGowan (OF)	1922–23
Hector Martinez (OF)	1962–63	Mark McGwire (1B)	1986–97
Marty Martinez (SS)	1972	Stuffy McInnis (1B)	1909–17
Ted Martinez (SS)	1975	Matty McIntyre (OF)	1901
Wedo Martini (P)	1935	Cody McKay (C)	2002
Bob Martyn (OF)	1957–59	Dave McKay (2B)	1980–82
Damon Mashore (OF)	1996–97	Tim McKeithan (P)	1932–34
Walt Masters (P)	1939	Bob McKinney (2B)	1901
Len Matarazzo (P)	1952	Rich McKinney (3B)	1973–77
Joe Mathes (2B)	1912	Denny McLain (P)	1972
Nelson Mathews (OF)	1964–65	Bo McLaughlin (P)	1981–82
T.J. Mathews (P)	1997–2001	Pat McLaughlin (P)	1940
Francisco Matos (2B)	1994	Mark McLemore (2B)	2004
Wid Matthews (OF)	1923	Jack McMahan (P)	1956

Jim McManus (1B)	1960	Paul Mitchell (P)	1976–77
Greg McMichael (P)	1999	Ralph Mitterling (OF)	1916
Billy McMillon (OF)	2001, 2003–04	Mike Mohler (P)	1993–98
Ken McMullen (3B)	1976	Izzy Molina (C)	1996–98
Eric McNair (SS)	1929–35, 1942	Rinty Monahan (P)	1953
Bob McNamara (3B)	1939	Rick Monday (OF)	1966–71
Rusty McNealy (DH)	1983	Aurelio Monteagudo (P)	1963–66
Bill McNulty (OF)	1969, 1972	Steve Montgomery (P)	1996–97
John McPherson (P)	1901	Bill Mooneyham (P)	1986
Jerry McQuaig (OF)	1934	Ferdie Moore (1B)	1914
George McQuinn (1B)	1946	Jimmy Moore (OF)	1930–31
Jim Mecir (P)	2000–04	Kelvin Moore (1B)	1981–83
Doc Medich (P)	1977	Kerwin Moore (OF)	1996
Bill Meehan (P)	1915	Mike Moore (P)	1989–92
Roy Meeker (P)	1923–24	Roy Moore (P)	1920–22
Adam Melhuse (C)	2003–06	Jose Morales (DH)	1973
Joe Mellana (3B)	1927	Herbie Moran (OF)	1908
Dave Melton (OF)	1956–58	Dave Morey (P)	1913
Frank Menechino (2B)	1999–2004	Cy Morgan (P)	1909–12
Orlando Mercado (C)	1988	Joe Morgan (2B)	1984
Henry Mercedes (C)	1992–93	Joe Morgan (3B)	1959
Charlie Metro (OF)	1944–45	Mike Morgan (P)	1978–79
Alex Metzler (OF)	1926	Tom Morgan (P)	1957
Billy Meyer (C)	1916–17	Doyt Morris (OF)	1937
Bob Meyer (P)	1964	Bill Morrisette (P)	1915–16
Dan Meyer (1B)	1982–85	Bud Morse (2B)	1929
Russ Meyer (P)	1959	Wally Moses (OF)	1935–41, 1949–51
Scott Meyer (C)	1978	Charlie Moss (C)	1934–36
Cass Michaels (2B)	1952–53	Don Mossi (P)	1965
Carl Miles (P)	1940	Mark Mulder (P)	2000–04
Dee Miles (OF)	1939–42	Jim Mullin (2B)	1904
Bing Miller (OF)	1922–26, 1928–34	Jake Munch (OF)	1918
Damian Miller (C)	2004	Pedro Munoz (OF)	1996
Rudy Miller (3B)	1929	Steve Mura (P)	1985
Billy Milligan (P)	1901	Danny Murphy (2B)	1902–13
Bill Mills (C)	1944	Dwayne Murphy (OF)	1978–87
Don Mincher (1B)	1970–72	Eddie Murphy (OF)	1912–15
Ray Miner (P)	1921	Mike Murphy (C)	1916
Craig Minetto (P)	1978–81	Morgan Murphy (C)	1901
Craig Mitchell (P)	1975–77	Joe Murray (P)	1950
Fred Mitchell (P)	1902	Larry Murray (OF)	1977–79
Kevin Mitchell (OF)	1998	Ray Murray (C)	1951–53

Glenn Myatt (C)	1920–21
Elmer Myers (P)	1915–18
Greg Myers (C)	2001–02
Joseph Myers (P)	1905

N

Jack Nabors (P)	1915–17
Bill Nagel (2B)	1939
Pete Naktenis (P)	1936
Jim Nash (P)	1966–69
Rollie Naylor (P)	1917–24
Troy Neel (DH)	1992–94
Mike Neill (OF)	1998
Gene Nelson (P)	1987–92
Lynn Nelson (P)	1937–39
Rob Nelson (1B)	1986–87
Jim Nettles (OF)	1981
Mike Neu (P)	2003
Jeff Newman (C)	1976–82
Bobo Newsom (P)	1944–46, 1952–53
Skeeter Newsome (SS)	1935–39
Simon Nicholls (SS)	1906–09
Bill Nicholson (OF)	1936
Al Niemiec (2B)	1936
Junior Noboa (2B)	1994
Pete Noonan (C)	1904
Irv Noren (OF)	1957
Fred Norman (P)	1962–63
Mike Norris (P)	1975–90
Billy North (OF)	1973–78
Joe Nossek (OF)	1966–67, 1969
Win Noyes (P)	1917, 1919
Edwin Nunez (P)	1993–94
Joe Nuxhall (P)	1961

O

Charlie O'Brien (C)	1985
Blue Moon Odom (P)	1964–75
John O'Donoghue (P)	1963–65
Curly Ogden (P)	1922–24
Jim Oglesby (1B)	1936
Rube Oldring (OF)	1906–18

Omar Olivares (P)	1999–2000
Harry O'Neill (P)	1922–23
Harry O'Neill (C)	1939
Steve Ontiveros (P)	1985–88, 1994–95
Mike Oquist (P)	1997–99
Billy Orr (SS)	1913–14
Jose Ortiz (2B)	2000–01
Roberto Ortiz (OF)	1950
Ossie Orwoll (P)	1928–29
Dan Osinski (P)	1962
Darrell Osteen (P)	1970
Bill Oster (P)	1954
Dave Otto (P)	1987–90
Bob Owchinko (P)	1981–82
Jack Owens (C)	1935
Doc Ozmer (P)	1923

P

Mitchell Page (DH)	1977–83
Sam Page (P)	1939
Jim Pagliaroni (C)	1968–69
Satchel Paige (P)	1965
Eddie Palmer (3B)	1917
Joe Palmisano (C)	1931
Jim Panther (P)	1971
Craig Paquette (3B)	1993–95
Tony Parisse (C)	1943–44
Ace Parker (SS)	1937–38
Dave Parker (OF)	1988–89
Roy Parmelee (P)	1939
Rube Parnham (P)	1916–17
Jeff Parrett (P)	1992
Bill Parsons (P)	1974
Joe Pate (P)	1926–27
Daryl Patterson (P)	1971
Mike Patterson (OF)	1981
Bill Patton (C)	1935
Jay Payton (OF)	2005–06
Hal Peck (OF)	1944–46
Jack Peerson (SS)	1935–36
Monte Peffer (SS)	1913
Carlos Pena (1B)	2002

Orlando Pena (P)	1962–65	Ray Poole (—)	1941–47
Roberto Pena (SS)	1970	Bo Porter (OF)	2000
Herb Pennock (P)	1912–15	Odie Porter (P)	1902
Bob Pepper (P)	1915	Arnie Portocarrero (P)	1954–57
Antonio Perez (2B)	2006	Leo Posada (OF)	1960–62
Marty Perez (SS)	1977–78	Nels Potter (P)	1938–41, 1948
Charlie Perkins (P)	1930	Vic Power (1B)	1954–58
Cy Perkins (C)	1915–30	Doc Powers (C)	1901–09
Jim Perry (P)	1975	Ike Powers (P)	1927–28
Scott Perry (P)	1918–21	Bobby Prescott (OF)	1961
Rick Peters (OF)	1983–86	Ariel Prieto (P)	1995–98, 2000
Rusty Peters (2B)	1936–38	Jim Pruett (C)	1944–45
Jim Peterson (P)	1931–33	George Puccinelli (OF)	1936
Dan Pfister (P)	1961–64		
Ken Phelps (DH)	1989–90	**Q**	
Dave Philley (OF)	1951–53	Jack Quinn (P)	1925–30
Tony Phillips (OF)	1982–89, 1999	Tad Quinn (P)	1902–03
Steve Phoenix (P)	1994–95	Luis Quinones (3B)	1983
Adam Piatt (OF)	2000–03	Jamie Quirk (C)	1989–92
Wiley Piatt (P)	1901		
Rob Picciolo (SS)	1977–82, 1985	**R**	
Val Picinich (C)	1916–17	Mike Raczka (P)	1992
Charlie Pick (2B)	1916	Hal Raether (P)	1954, 1957
Ollie Pickering (OF)	1903–04	Tim Raines (OF)	1999
Tony Pierce (P)	1967–68	Chuck Rainey (P)	1984
William Pierson (P)	1918–24	Ed Rakow (P)	1961–63
Joe Pignatano (C)	1961	Milt Ramirez (SS)	1979
Al Pilarcik (OF)	1956, 1961	Willie Randolph (2B)	1990
Squiz Pillion (P)	1915	Vic Raschi (P)	1955
Horacio Pina (P)	1973	Morrie Rath (2B)	1909–10
Ed Pinnance (P)	1903	Jon Ratliff (P)	1999–2000
Cotton Pippen (P)	1939	Carl Ray (P)	1915–16
Jim Pisoni (OF)	1956–57	Randy Ready (2B)	1992
Gaylen Pitts (3B)	1974–75	Britt Reames (P)	2005
Juan Pizarro (P)	1969	Mark Redman (P)	2004
Eddie Plank (P)	1901–14	Howie Reed (P)	1958–60
Phil Plantier (OF)	1996	Al Reiss (SS)	1932
Don Plarski (OF)	1955	Jim Reninger (P)	1938–39
Rance Pless (1B)	1956	Steve Renko (P)	1978
Eric Plunk (P)	1986–89	Bill Renna (OF)	1954–56
Luis Polonia (OF)	1987–89	Roger Repoz (OF)	1966–67
Jim Poole (1B)	1925–27	Otto Rettig (P)	1922

Todd Revenig (P)	1992	Braggo Roth (OF)	1919
Dave Revering (1B)	1978–81	Jack Rothrock (OF)	1937
Carlos Reyes (P)	1994–97	Mike Rouse (SS)	2006
Tommie Reynolds (OF)	1963–65, 1969	Harland Rowe (3B)	1916
Arthur Rhodes (P)	2004	Chuck Rowland (C)	1923
Gordon Rhodes (P)	1936	Emil Roy (P)	1933
Paul Richards (C)	1935	Dick Rozek (P)	1953–54
Jack Richardson (P)	1915–16	Al Rubeling (3B)	1940–41
Ken Richardson (2B)	1942	Joe Rudi (OF)	1968–76, 1982
Don Richmond (3B)	1941–47	Joe Rullo (2B)	1943–44
Harry Riconda (3B)	1923–24	Jeff Russell (P)	1992
Brad Rigby (P)	1997–99	Lefty Russell (P)	1910–12
Dave Righetti (P)	1994	Mickey Rutner (3B)	1947
Jose Rijo (P)	1985–87	Rob Ryan (OF)	2001
Ernest Riles (SS)	1991		
Ricardo Rincon (P)	2002–05	**S**	
Bob Rinker (C)	1950	Kirk Saarloos (P)	2004–06
Jimmy Ripple (OF)	1943	Olmedo Saenz (1B)	1999–2002
Jim Rivera (OF)	1961	Tom Saffell (OF)	1955
Bip Roberts (2B)	1998	Johnny Sain (P)	1955
Ray Roberts (P)	1919	Lenn Sakata (2B)	1986
Jim Robertson (C)	1954–55	Roger Salmon (P)	1912
Sherry Robertson (OF)	1952	Gus Salve (P)	1908
Bruce Robinson (C)	1978	Ed Samcoff (2B)	1951
Eddie Robinson (1B)	1953, 1956	Alejandro Sanchez (OF)	1987
Floyd Robinson (OF)	1968	John Sanders (—)	1965
Ben Rochefort (1B)	1914	Ken Sanders (P)	1964, 1966, 1968
Rick Rodriguez (P)	1986–87	Scott Sanderson (P)	1990
Roberto Rodriguez (P)	1967, 1970	Charlie Sands (DH)	1975
Oscar Roettger (1B)	1932	Tommy Sandt (SS)	1975–76
Kenny Rogers (P)	1997–99	Jack Sanford (P)	1967
Tom Rogers (P)	1919	Manny Sanguillen (C)	1977
Jim Roland (P)	1969–72	F.P. Santangelo (OF)	2001
Dutch Romberger (P)	1954	Jose Santiago (P)	1956
Eddie Rommel (P)	1920–32	Jose Santiago (P)	1963–65
Matt Roney (P)	2006	Scott Sauerbeck (P)	2006
Phil Roof (C)	1966–69	Rusty Saunders (OF)	1927
Buddy Rosar (C)	1945–49	Rich Sauveur (P)	2000
Santiago Rosario (1B)	1965	Bob Savage (P)	1942–48
Mike Rose (C)	2004	Steve Sax (2B)	1994
Larry Rosenthal (OF)	1944–45	Jeff Schaefer (SS)	1994
Buck Ross (P)	1936–41	Wally Schang (C)	1913–17, 1930

Rube Schauer (P)	1917	Dick Siebert (1B)	1938–45
Heinie Scheer (2B)	1922–23	Sonny Siebert (P)	1975
Carl Scheib (P)	1943–54	Ruben Sierra (OF)	1992–95
Jim Schelle (P)	1939	Frank Sigafoos (3B)	1926
Red Schillings (P)	1922	Al Sima (P)	1954
Biff Schlitzer (P)	1908–09	Al Simmons (OF)	1924–32, 1940–41, 1944
Ossee Schreckengost (C)	1902–08	Harry Simpson (OF)	1955–59
Hack Schumann (P)	1906	Matt Sinatro (C)	1987–88
Randy Schwartz (1B)	1965–66	Chris Singleton (OF)	2003
Jerry Schypinski (SS)	1955	Frank Skaff (1B)	1943
Dick Scott (SS)	1989	Lou Skizas (OF)	1956–57
Rodney Scott (2B)	1977	John Slappey (P)	1920
Marco Scutaro (2B)	2004–06	Enos Slaughter (OF)	1955–56
Diego Segui (P)	1962–65, 1967–68, 1970–72	Lou Sleater (P)	1955
Socks Seibold (P)	1915–19	Joe Slusarski (P)	1991–93
Kevin Seitzer (3B)	1993	Aaron Small (P)	1996–98
Scott Service (P)	2000	Jim Small (OF)	1958
Jimmy Sexton (SS)	1981–82	Dave Smith (P)	1938–39
Socks Seybold (OF)	1901–08	Eddie Smith (P)	1936–39
Art Shamsky (OF)	1972	Hal Smith (C)	1956–59
Bill Shanner (P)	1920	Harry Smith (C)	1901
Red Shannon (2B)	1917–21	Mark Smith (P)	1983
Billy Shantz (C)	1954–55	Mayo Smith (OF)	1945
Bobby Shantz (P)	1949–56	Red Smith (SS)	1925
Ralph Sharman (OF)	1917	Syd Smith (C)	1908
Shag Shaughnessy (OF)	1908	Roger Smithberg (P)	1993–94
Jeff Shaver (P)	1988	Bernie Snyder (2B)	1935
Bob Shaw (P)	1961	Brian Snyder (P)	1989
Don Shaw (P)	1972	Russ Snyder (OF)	1959–60
Bob Shawkey (P)	1913–15	Lary Sorensen (P)	1984
Red Shea (P)	1918	Elias Sosa (P)	1978
Dave Shean (2B)	1906	Mark Souza (P)	1980
Tom Sheehan (P)	1915–16	Steve Sparks (P)	2003
Rollie Sheldon (P)	1965–66	Tris Speaker (OF)	1928
Scott Sheldon (3B)	1997	Jim Spencer (1B)	1981–82
Ed Sherling (—)	1924	Stan Sperry (2B)	1938
Joe Sherman (P)	1915	Bob Spicer (P)	1955–56
Tex Shirley (P)	1941–42	Scott Spiezio (1B)	1996–99
Charlie Shoemaker (2B)	1961–64	Ed Sprague (P)	1968–69
Bill Shores (P)	1928–31	Ed Sprague (3B)	1998–99
Eric Show (P)	1991	Bill Stafford (P)	1966–67
Norm Siebern (1B)	1960–63	Steve Staggs (2B)	1978

Larry Stahl (OF)	1964–66
Tuck Stainback (OF)	1946
Matt Stairs (OF)	1996–2000
Gerry Staley (P)	1961
George Staller (OF)	1943
Fred Stanley (SS)	1981–82
Mike Stanley (C)	2000
Farmer Steelman (C)	1901–02
Blake Stein (P)	1998–99
Irv Stein (P)	1932
Terry Steinbach (C)	1986–96
Bill Stellbauer (OF)	1916
Gene Stephens (OF)	1961–62
Bill Stewart (OF)	1955
Dave Stewart (P)	1986–92, 1995
Wes Stock (P)	1964–67
Art Stokes (P)	1925
Ron Stone (OF)	1966
Todd Stottlemyre (P)	1995–96
Paul Strand (OF)	1924
Huston Street (P)	2005–06
Amos Strunk (OF)	1908–17, 1919–20, 1924
Tom Sturdivant (P)	1959, 1963–64
Dean Sturgis (C)	1914
Lena Styles (C)	1919–21
Ken Suarez (C)	1966–67
Pete Suder (2B)	1941–43, 1946–55
Haywood Sullivan (C)	1961–63
Jim Sullivan (P)	1921–22
Homer Summa (OF)	1929–30
Champ Summers (OF)	1974
Don Sutton (P)	1985
Larry Sutton (OF)	2002
Dale Sveum (SS)	1993
Buck Sweeney (OF)	1914
Bob Swift (C)	1942–43
Nick Swisher (OF)	2004–06

T

Jerry Tabb (1B)	1977–78
John Taff (P)	1913
Fred Talbot (P)	1965–66, 1969–70

Tim Talton (C)	1966–67
Jeff Tam (P)	2000–02
Danny Tartabull (OF)	1995
Jose Tartabull (OF)	1962–66, 1969–70
Arlas Taylor (P)	1921
Billy Taylor (P)	1994–99
Harry Taylor (P)	1957
Joe Taylor (OF)	1954
Miguel Tejada (SS)	1997–2003
Dave Telgheder (P)	1996–98
Tom Tellmann (P)	1985
Gene Tenace (C)	1969–76
Ralph Terry (P)	1957–59, 1966
Wayne Terwilliger (2B)	1959–60
Mickey Tettleton (C)	1984–87
Dave Thies (P)	1963
Bud Thomas (P)	1937–39
Charles Thomas (OF)	2005
Frank Thomas (DH)	2006
Fred Thomas (3B)	1919–20
Ira Thomas (C)	1909–15
Kite Thomas (OF)	1952–53
Gary Thomasson (OF)	1978
Harry Thompson (P)	1919
Shag Thompson (OF)	1914–16
Tim Thompson (C)	1956–57
Buck Thrasher (OF)	1916–17
Marv Throneberry (1B)	1960–61
Rusty Tillman (OF)	1986
Eric Tipton (OF)	1939–41
Joe Tipton (C)	1950–52
Pat Tobin (P)	1941
Jim Todd (P)	1975–76, 1979
Phil Todt (1B)	1931
Dick Tomanek (P)	1958–59
Andy Tomberlin (OF)	1995
Ron Tompkins (P)	1965
Rupe Toppin (P)	1962
Pablo Torrealba (P)	1977
Mike Torrez (P)	1976–77, 1984
Cesar Tovar (OF)	1975–76
Bob Trice (P)	1953–55

Jerry Willard (C)	1986–87	Dooley Womack (P)	1970
Al Williams (P)	1937–38	Doc Wood (SS)	1923
Billy Williams (OF)	1975–76	Jason Wood (1B)	1998
Dib Williams (2B)	1930–35	Mike Wood (P)	2003
Dick Williams (OF)	1959–60	Darrell Woodard (2B)	1978
Don Williams (P)	1962	Gary Woods (OF)	1976
Earl Williams (C)	1977	Fred Worden (P)	1914
George Williams (2B)	1964	Tim Worrell (P)	1998–99
George Williams (C)	1995–97	Rich Wortham (P)	1983
Mark Williams (OF)	1977	Ed Wright (P)	1952
Marsh Williams (P)	1916	Taffy Wright (OF)	1949
Dale Willis (P)	1963	John Wyatt (P)	1961–66, 1969
Lefty Willis (P)	1925–27	Weldon Wyckoff (P)	1913–16
Whitey Wilshere (P)	1934–36	Hank Wyse (P)	1950–51
Bill Wilson (OF)	1954–55		
Highball Wilson (P)	1902	**Y**	
Jack Wilson (P)	1934	Keiichi Yabu (P)	2005
Jim Wilson (P)	1949	George Yankowski (C)	1942
Tom Wilson (C)	2001	Rube Yarrison (P)	1922
Willie Wilson (OF)	1991–92	Carroll Yerkes (P)	1927–29
Snake Wiltse (P)	1901–02	Lefty York (P)	1919
Gordie Windhorn (OF)	1962	Rudy York (1B)	1948
Jason Windsor (P)	2006	Elmer Yoter (3B)	1921
Al Wingo (OF)	1919	Curt Young (P)	1983–91, 1993
Ed Wingo (C)	1920	Ernie Young (OF)	1994–97
Hank Winston (P)	1933	Matt Young (P)	1989
Alan Wirth (P)	1978–80	Ralph Young (2B)	1922
Jay Witasick (P)	1996–98, 2005–06	Eddie Yount (OF)	1937
Ron Witmeyer (1B)	1991		
Bobby Witt (P)	1992–94	**Z**	
Whitey Witt (OF)	1916–21	Tom Zachary (P)	1918
Steve Wojciechowski (P)	1995–97	Joe Zapustas (OF)	1933
John Wojcik (OF)	1962–64	Gus Zernial (OF)	1951–57
Lefty Wolf (P)	1921	Jimmy Zinn (P)	1919
Chuck Wolfe (P)	1923	Barry Zito (P)	2000–06
Roger Wolff (P)	1941–43	Sam Zoldak (P)	1951–52

Williams Would Be in the Hall if He'd Been in New York

"'Gentlemen,' he began, 'some of you...'" Bergman, Ron. *Mustache Gang*. New York: Dell Publishing, 1973.

"If that's God's plan..." Travers, Steven. "Williams Would Be in Hall if He'd Been in New York," *The* (San Francisco) *Examiner,* March 1, 2001.

Cap'n Sal

"The only reason [Joe] Rudi and me..." Libby, Bill. *Charlie O. & the Angry A's*. New York: Doubleday, 1975.

"I wasn't as spectacular as..." Libby, Bill. *Charlie O. & the Angry A's*. New York: Doubleday, 1975.

"I don't stir up..." Libby, Bill. *Charlie O. & the Angry A's*. New York: Doubleday, 1975.

Jax

"Bryant smiled, looked away from me..." Travers, Steven. *September 1970: One Night, Two Teams, and the Game That Changed a Nation*. Colorado Springs, CO: Taylor Trade Publishers, 2007.

"I knew he didn't mean any harm..." Jackson, Reggie, with Mike Lupica. *Reggie*. New York: Random House, 1984.

"'Yessir,' added Bear, 'if I could just...'" Travers, Steven. "When Legends Played," *StreetZebra,* September 1999.

"I think we could find..." Jackson, Reggie, with Mike Lupica. *Reggie*. New York: Random House, 1984.

"If the A's had been kept together..." Jackson, Reggie. *Rebels of Oakland*. HBO documentary hosted by Tom Hanks, 2005.

The "Mustache Gang"

"This is a game..." Michelson, Herb. *Charlie O.* New York: Bobbs-Merrill, 1975.

The Hairs versus the Squares

"The secret here is they underrate..." Libby, Bill. *Charlie O. & the Angry A's*. New York: Doubleday, 1975.

"looked over at the hairy..." Angell, Roger. *Five Seasons: A Baseball Companion*. New York: Simon & Schuster, 1977.

Reggie Takes Charge
"Well, that means he can't give you..." Libby, Bill, and Vida Blue. *Vida.* Englewood Cliffs, NJ: Prentice-Hall, 1972.
"You'd sit down with Charlie..." Jackson, Reggie, with Mike Lupica. *Reggie.* New York: Random House, 1984.
"so good blind people come to the park..." Devaney, John. *Tom Seaver: An Intimate Portrait.* New York: Popular Library, 1974.

A Rare Thing
"I don't think anyone means..." Libby, Bill. *Charlie O. & the Angry A's.* New York: Doubleday, 1975.
"not getting a lot of players..." Libby, Bill. *Charlie O. & the Angry A's.* New York: Doubleday, 1975.
"Leo believed we should eat..." Libby, Bill. *Charlie O. & the Angry A's.* New York: Doubleday, 1975.
"The guys can kid me..." Libby, Bill. *Charlie O. & the Angry A's.* New York: Doubleday, 1975.

Son of a Preacher Man
"couldn't manage a meat market" Libby, Bill. *Charlie O. & the Angry A's.* New York: Doubleday, 1975.

Catfish
"What good are they?..." Libby, Bill. *Charlie O. & the Angry A's.* New York: Doubleday, 1975.
"I did fish a lot..." Libby, Bill. *Charlie O. & the Angry A's.* New York: Doubleday, 1975.
"Hunter knows what he's doing..." Michelson, Herb. *Charlie O.* New York: Bobbs-Merrill, 1975.
"I don't need a lot of glory..." Michelson, Herb. *Charlie O.* New York: Bobbs-Merrill, 1975.

Silent Joe
"From the age of five, all I wanted..." Libby, Bill. *Charlie O. & the Angry A's.* New York: Doubleday, 1975.
"was so excited he was coming..." Bergman, Ron. *Mustache Gang.* New York: Dell Publishing, 1973.

"I owe everything I have..." Bergman, Ron. *Mustache Gang*. New York: Dell Publishing, 1973.

"I say we should dispose..." Jackson, Reggie, with Mike Lupica. *Reggie*. New York: Random House, 1984.

"It's Hold 'Em Rollie Fingers Time"

"Rollie was too dumb to know any better..." Travers, Steven. "Patriot Games: A Conversation with Rick Monday," *StreetZebra*, June 1999.

"Call your stock broker...." Travers, Steven. "Patriot Games: A Conversation with Rick Monday." *StreetZebra*, June 1999.

Billy Ball

"Billy was my favorite manager." Henderson, Rickey, with John Shea. *Off Base: Confessions of a Thief*. New York: HarperCollins, 1992.

Completing What They Started

"Hell no, they're not..." *Rebels of Oakland*. HBO documentary hosted by Tom Hanks, 2005.

Hot Dog

"Yes, I am a hot dog...." Henderson, Rickey, with John Shea. *Off Base: Confessions of a Thief*. New York: HarperCollins, 1992.

"I knew a lot of guys better..." Henderson, Rickey, with John Shea. *Off Base: Confessions of a Thief*. New York: HarperCollins, 1992.

"If I didn't get this..." Henderson, Rickey, with John Shea. *Off Base: Confessions of a Thief*. New York: HarperCollins, 1992.

The "Bash Brothers"

"How could they name such..." Stier, Kit. "Metrodome Gets Less Than Rave Reviews." *The Oakland Tribune*, April 14, 1982.

October 1989

"After his 40/40 year..." Dickey, Glenn. *Champions*. Chicago: Triumph Books, 2002.

"What Rickey needed wasn't always..." Fimrite, Ron. *Three Weeks in October*. Woodford Publishing, 1990.

"We knew going in..." Dickey, Glenn. *Champions*. Chicago: Triumph Books, 2002.

"Big Mac"
"That's just not a part of..." Travers, Steven. *Barry Bonds: Baseball's Superman*. Champaign, IL: Sports Publishing, 2002.

Stew
"We had bad chemistry..." Dickey, Glenn. *Champions*. Chicago: Triumph Books, 2002.

"I had been with a couple..." Dickey, Glenn. *Champions*. Chicago: Triumph Books, 2002.

"That made him a three-pitch pitcher..." Dickey, Glenn. *Champions*. Chicago: Triumph Books, 2002.

"Roger and I had some..." Dickey, Glenn. *Champions*. Chicago: Triumph Books, 2002.

Shakespeare's Closer
"It knocked me down..." Dickey, Glenn. *Champions*. Chicago: Triumph Books, 2002.

"Eckersley was driven by his fear..." Travers, Steven. "A King Walks amongst Us." *The* (San Francisco) *Examiner*, May 18, 2001.

The Clubhouse Lawyer
"I don't need to look..." Bouton, Jim. *Ball Four*. New York: World Press, 1970.

"That season, we had..." Dickey, Glenn. *Champions*. Chicago: Triumph Books, 2002.

A King Walked among Us
"I always liked to talk..." Travers, Steven. "A King Walks amongst Us," *The* (San Francisco) *Examiner*, May 15, 2001.

"Davis is a fascinating man..." Travers, Steven. "A King Walks amongst Us." *The* (San Francisco) *Examiner*, May 18, 2001.

"Sid Gillman was the real force..." Travers, Steven. "A King Walks amongst Us." *The* (San Francisco) *Examiner,* May 18, 2001.

"It's better than saying..." Travers, Steven. "A King Walks amongst Us." *The* (San Francisco) *Examiner,* May 18, 2001.

"Ken Stabler was a delight..." Travers, Steven. "A King Walks amongst Us." *The* (San Francisco) *Examiner,* May 18, 2001.

Hudson and the A's Had the Time of Their Lives

All quotes in this chapter are from: Travers, Steven. "A's, Hudson Having Time of Their Lives," *The* (San Francisco) *Examiner,* April 1, 2001.

Mulder Stepped Up

"Michigan State's real good..." Travers, Steven. "Mulder Steps It Up," *The* (San Francisco) *Examiner,* March 29, 2001.

"There's always been something..." Urban, Mychael. *Aces: The Last Season on the Mound with the Oakland A's Big Three.* Hoboken, New Jersey: John Wiley & Sons, 2005.

"From the moment he came..." Urban, Mychael. *Aces: The Last Season on the Mound with the Oakland A's Big Three.* Hoboken, New Jersey: John Wiley & Sons, 2005.

"Why would I care..." Urban, Mychael. *Aces: The Last Season on the Mound with the Oakland A's Big Three.* Hoboken, New Jersey: John Wiley & Sons, 2005.

Zito

"He's the real deal." Travers, Steven. "Ex-Trojan Zito Is Big A's Prospect," *StreetZebra,* March 2000.

"SC seemed out of my reach..." Travers, Steven. "Zito Key to A's Resurgence," *The* (San Francisco) *Examiner,* February 8, 2001.

"Santa Barbara just wasn't..." Travers, Steven. "Zito Key to A's Resurgence." *The* (San Francisco) *Examiner,* February 8, 2001.

"I work hard because..." Travers, Steven. "Ex-Trojan Zito Is Big A's Prospect." *StreetZebra,* March 2000.

Boy Genius

"Sandy told me when I became his assistant…" Lewis, Michael. *Moneyball.* New York: W.W. Norton, 2003.

2005–2006: A New Era

"Everybody left it out on the field." DiGiovanna, Mike. "Tigers Walk Off with a Sweep." *Los Angeles Times,* October 15, 2006.